SAS
BATTLE
READY

SAS BATTLE READY

TRUE STORIES FROM MEMORABLE MISSIONS AROUND THE WORLD

DOMINIC UTTON

Michael O'Mara Books Limited

First published in Great Britain in 2023 by
Michael O'Mara Books Limited
9 Lion Yard
Tremadoc Road
London SW4 7NQ

Copyright © Michael O'Mara Books Limited 2023

All rights reserved. You may not copy, store, distribute, transmit,
reproduce or otherwise make available this publication (or any part of
it) in any form, or by any means (electronic, digital, optical, mechanical,
photocopying, recording or otherwise), without the prior written
permission of the publisher. Any person who does any unauthorized act
in relation to this publication may be liable to criminal prosecution and
civil claims for damages.

A CIP catalogue record for this book is available from the British Library.

This product is made of material from well-managed, FSC®-certified
forests and other controlled sources. The manufacturing processes
conform to the environmental regulations of the country of origin.

ISBN: 978-1-78929-529-0 in paperback print format
ISBN: 978-1-78929-537-5 in ebook format

1 2 3 4 5 6 7 8 9 10

Designed and typeset by D23
Cover picture credit: guvendemir / Getty Images
Printed and bound by CPI Group (UK) Ltd, Croydon, CR0 4YY

www.mombooks.com

CONTENTS

PART 2: GLOBAL THREATS

PART 3: POST 9/11

INTRODUCTION

THEY ARE THE BEST of the best. For over eighty years the Special Air Service has been a name synonymous with bold, daring commando raids carried out with a courage, dedication and skill unmatched by any other fighting force in the world.

In that time the elite unit has fought in wars, combated terrorism, rescued hostages and executed undercover (and often unreported) operations across the globe – from the deserts of Libya in 1941 to the mountains and forests of occupied Europe, the jungles of Borneo, Malaysia and Sierra Leone, the frozen islands of the South Atlantic, the streets of Northern Ireland, the burning wastes of Iraq, the deadly cave complexes of Afghanistan ... often outnumbered, frequently outgunned, but rarely, if ever, defeated.

Theirs is a history formed of three ages. First conceived by a maverick lieutenant frustrated by the British army's apparent inability to halt German Field Marshal Rommel's advance across North Africa, the SAS began as a tiny, dedicated band of troublemakers, waging a campaign of stealth and sabotage against the Nazis, but in the years after the war it evolved into a crack force capable of taking on any enemy, in any situation.

Following the defeat of Nazi Germany in 1945, the unit was even disbanded, before being re-formed again just two years later.

Operations around the globe followed, protecting British and Commonwealth territories, defending against and frustrating communist and insurgent threats, combating terrorism, both domestic and foreign. More recently, the SAS has adapted again, deployed in Iraq and Afghanistan to stem a rising tide of fanaticism directed at the West, in which innocent civilians have often been the targets of terrorist extremists.

In that time some of their exploits have become legendary. Images of balaclava-clad troopers smashing through the windows of the Iranian embassy in 1980 to liberate hostages have become part of British folklore; books like Andy McNab's *Bravo Two Zero*, telling the story of an ill-fated patrol in the first Gulf War, have topped the bestseller charts; and TV series like the BBC's *SAS Rogue Heroes* have proved hits worldwide.

These adventures are rightly celebrated, but they do not constitute the whole tale.

The full story of the world's most feared elite fighting unit remains hidden, much of it classified, names redacted, details subject to the strictures of national security.

Over the following pages, that history – or as much of it as possible – will be revealed. Through dramatic accounts of the SAS's forty greatest missions, the courage, resourcefulness, skill, audacity and sheer bloody-minded daring of the unit – and of the men who serve in it – will come to life. Sometimes shocking, sometimes scarcely believable, but always inspiring, each of the operations stands as a testament to those who took part in it. Put together, they are nothing less than awe-inspiring.

Becoming a part of the SAS is an ambition most members of the armed forces hold – but only a handful make the cut.

Candidates are put through a gruelling selection process designed to push their strength, endurance and mental toughness to the limit, and fewer than 10 per cent will complete it.

First comes the 'hills' phase. For three weeks in the Brecon Beacons and Black Hills of South Wales, the candidates will carry increasingly heavy bergens (the special forces rucksack) over a series of gruelling hikes with no instruction or encouragement from officers, culminating in the 'long drag' – a 40-mile (64-km) yomp carrying 55 pounds (25 kg) on their back with a time limit of twenty-four hours.

Make it through the hills and the candidates are dropped into Belize, where they are put through the basics of survival in the jungle, learning not only to live in the wild for weeks without aid or backup, but to carry out patrols and missions in the harshest conditions.

Barely two dozen of the 125 intake will still remain to take on the third, and most mentally challenging, final phase. Escape, Evasion and Tactical Questioning recreates operations behind enemy lines ... and what happens when things go wrong. For three days the candidates are set loose in unfamiliar terrain, charged with making their way to a series of checkpoints while escaping detection from a pursuing force.

Whether successful or not, they are all then subjected to 'tactical questioning'. Their mental strength is pushed to the limit as they are screamed at, humiliated, denied sleep and forced to stand in 'stress positions' for hours on end while white noise is blasted at them. Any candidate who fails to answer questions with only their name, rank, serial number and date of birth – or with 'I'm sorry but I cannot answer that question' – fails instantly.

On average just ten of each set of candidates ever receive the famous winged dagger insignia of the SAS. There's a reason they're the best.

The forty true tales of SAS missions in this book illustrate just how important this rigorous selection process is – and how these unique skills, adaptability, self-reliance and combination of physical and mental toughness have made this special force the most feared and respected in the world.

If the book also reads like a history of eight decades of global conflict, insurgency and terrorism, that is no accident. As wars, unrest, and ever-more extreme acts of terrorism continue across the world, rest assured that the SAS are out there, whether we get to hear of it or not.

This is the story of how the vision of a handful of half-mad mavericks led to the formation of a world-famous fighting force. The story of men who dared ... and won.

PART 1

FORGED IN WAR

OPERATION SQUATTER

LIBYA, 16 NOVEMBER 1941

THE MOST FAMOUS elite fighting unit in the world was born out of desperation – and began in failure. But as the saying goes, it's not about how many times you get knocked down, it's about how many times you get back up again. The very first mission for the newly formed Special Air Service was a disaster, but it only made the men behind the SAS more determined to prove their worth.

In July 1941, the British army were under the sword in North Africa. The gains the Allies had made the previous winter had been all but wiped out by Field Marshal Rommel's reinvigorated Afrika Korps; the aggression and ambition of his spring counter-offensive had pushed the British back to the Libyan city of Tobruk: trapped between the desert and the sea, the Allies would endure a siege that was to last 241 days from April until November 1941.

From this perilous position came a bold plan – and a man with the drive and vision to make it happen.

Lieutenant Archibald David Stirling of the Scots Guards was just twenty-five when he first formulated his idea for what would become the SAS. His concept was simple: in the face of overwhelming German tank and air superiority, small raiding parties of commandos would penetrate deep behind enemy lines, use stealth and surprise to infiltrate bases and airfields, and in fast, deadly, smash-and-grab raids, destroy aircraft, armament and fuel supplies, before disappearing again, as quickly and mysteriously as they had appeared.

According to Stirling, such tactics meant not only that a few men could inflict more damage – with less risk – than in a traditional attack, and not only that multiple targets could be hit simultaneously, but also that the fear and confusion such apparently undefendable operations created would help break the enemy's morale and dispel the myth of invincibility that had grown around Rommel.

Stirling presented his proposals to General Neil Ritchie, Deputy Commander of British Forces in the Middle East – even breaking into his headquarters in Cairo so as to bypass the traditional chain of command. Ritchie was impressed enough to excuse the unconventional approach, and persuaded Commander-in-Chief General Sir Claude Auchinleck to allow Stirling to form his special operations unit.

On 28 August 1941, L Detachment, Special Air Service Brigade – so called to mislead German intelligence that the unit was part of a greater parachute brigade – was officially raised, with Stirling, now promoted to captain, at its head. Under his command were five officers and sixty other men, drawn from commando units and selected for their strength and bravery. They would become known as 'The Originals'.

The new force was to have just a few months' training before embarking on its debut operation, codenamed Squatter, slated for 16 November.

◆ ◆ ◆

Operation Squatter did not fail because of a lack of military intelligence, ability or bravery, nor due to the superiority of Rommel's forces. It fell victim to the very thing that Captain Stirling was counting on in his favour: the brutal, unforgiving conditions of the desert itself.

On paper at least, the plan was sound, and encapsulated all of the strengths and advantages of the small raiding force that Stirling had outlined to General Auchinleck a few months before. His men were to parachute deep behind enemy lines, make their way by foot across 10 miles (16 km) of desert, and after laying up during the heat of the day, use the cover of night to penetrate the German airfields at Gazala and Timimi, some 50 miles (80 km) west of Tobruk. At one minute to midnight, the raiders would slip past the guards and stealthily plant bombs on as many of the planes as they could. The fuses would be lit at precisely 00.15, and Stirling's men would disappear back into the wild as all hell broke loose behind them.

Another gruelling 34-mile (55-km) hike inland through the night and following day would take them to the rendezvous point, at a remote track called the Trig-al-Abd, where they would be met by a party from the Long Range Desert Group, a deep-penetration reconnaissance unit.

To Stirling's eyes, the very thing that made the mission difficult was also its major strength. Rommel considered the desert itself to be a natural defence – launching any kind of significant attack on his airfields would mean leading a major force across countless miles of unforgiving terrain, a vast, featureless wilderness with little or no vegetation or natural cover, and scored with shallow, dried-up riverbeds called 'wadis'. During the day the heat was searing, the nights were freezing, and sudden storms could materialize dangerously quickly and seemingly out of nowhere, the wind whipping the sand into a stinging, blinding, impassable wall, with violent downpours flooding the wadis.

Such was Rommel's confidence in the desert, he left his airfields largely unprotected from ground attack – and ripe, reasoned Stirling, for the taking.

But the Western Desert did not earn its brutal reputation lightly – a lesson the men of the newly formed SAS were to learn to their cost.

At a little after 19.00 hours on 16 November, Stirling and fifty-four hand-picked men boarded five Bristol Bombay transport aircraft for the two-hour flight from the Egyptian base of Kaboush to the drop zone. Stirling had overall command, with the rest of his force divided into sections led by his two most senior officers, Lieutenant Jock Lewes and Lieutenant Paddy Mayne. Lewes was to target the Gazala base; Mayne to take out Timimi. Both men would go on to become legendary figures in the SAS.

The men travelled light: this was a hunting mission and speed and stealth were key. Each wore desert shirts and shorts and equipment was kept to a minimum – bare rations of biscuits, raisins, cheese and chocolate, a revolver, grenades, maps, a compass, and an entrenching tool. For roughly every two men, a canister would also be dropped, containing the crucial explosives, as well as spare ammunition, blankets and further rations.

Things began to go awry almost immediately. As the planes prepared to take off, reports came in of a storm blowing up almost directly over the drop zone, with winds of up to thirty knots. Flying in such conditions would be perilous enough –

parachuting into them even more dangerous. It was a do-or-die moment for Stirling. Should he abort the mission or continue?

He made the call: the SAS would jump.

It was the wrong call.

Battling poor visibility and rapidly deteriorating conditions, the lumbering Bristol Bombays struggled to maintain their flight paths, and were soon spotted by enemy anti-aircraft positions. Under heavy flak, one of the transports was shot down, with the loss of all fifteen men on board. Before firing a single shot in anger, the SAS had lost nearly a quarter of its force.

The remaining men did not fare much better. Jumping blind into the storm, the separate units were scattered miles from the drop zone. Worse, as they plunged through the darkness and the wind, many of their parachutes failed to open properly. Thrown around like rag dolls, the men hit the ground hard and were then dragged along the rocky desert floor; ankles turned, bones snapped, skin shredded.

A similar fate befell the canisters containing the vital explosives – many had either smashed on impact or been blown wildly off course, impossible to find.

Stirling, Mayne and Lewes all survived the landing with little more than cuts and bruises, and – now hopelessly cut off from each other – each set about trying to get the mission back on track. Of the three commanders, only Jock Lewes still had his full complement of men: Paddy Mayne was down to eight (with only enough food for four), and Stirling's unit was so badly hit that only he and one other man, Sergeant Bob Tait, were able to walk at all. Nevertheless, showing the kind of grim determination in the face of overwhelming odds that would go on to define the

SAS, they each separately resolved to continue, and after gathering what they could from the scattered and smashed canisters, set off north towards their targets.

As the storm intensified – it would later be described by *Daily Mail* war correspondent Alexander Clifford as 'the most spectacular thunderstorm within local memory' – Stirling and Tait were forced to turn back almost immediately for fear of becoming hopelessly disoriented. Lewes and his men marched through the night, but as dawn broke it became clear they had landed at least a dozen miles (19 km) south of the intended drop zone. With conditions worsening, he too made the decision to abort the mission. In *The SAS in World War II: An Illustrated History*, author Gavin Mortimer quotes an excerpt from the diary of one of the troopers, Lance Sergeant Jeff Du Vivier: 'The lightning was terrific,' he wrote. 'And how it rained! The compass was going round in circles. We were getting nowhere. And we were wallowing up to our knees in water. I remember seeing tortoises swimming about.'

Paddy Mayne fared a little better. He and his eight men managed to march within 6 miles (9.5 km) of Timimi airfield, before laying up in a wadi at dawn. What followed was the first example of what the SAS would later call 'hard routine' – entrenched for hours in deeply uncomfortable conditions, soaked by the rain, scorched by the sun, hungry and thirsty and nursing injuries, waiting for the signal to attack.

The signal never came. The storm had briefly abated during the day, but by the afternoon it returned with a vengeance. As the rain increased in ferocity, the wadi the men were sheltering in became a pool, and then a stream, and eventually a torrent. And it was not only the men who were soaked: the deluge had ruined the fuses needed to set off the bombs. Even if they could have made it into the airfield, they no longer had the capability to carry out their attack. Reluctantly, Paddy Mayne became the last man to abandon the mission.

It took another two days of arduous marching south to make it to the rendezvous point at Trig-al-Abd, where Lewes's men had arrived shortly before. Just hours later they were joined by Stirling and Tait. The depleted force waited a further eight hours for any stragglers before taking the agonizing decision to leave.

Of the fifty-five men who had set off from Kaboush on the evening of 16 November, just twenty-two returned. Captain Stirling's crack new special operations force had, in a stroke, lost getting on for two-thirds of its men, killed, missing or captured, without inflicting a single enemy casualty. Operation Squatter had, by almost every measure, been a catastrophic failure.

In the face of such humiliation, most men would have given up. Not Stirling – and not the men of the SAS, either. Within a month, L Detachment, Special Air Service Brigade would return to occupied Libya – with spectacular results.

TAMET AIRFIELD

LIBYA, 14 DECEMBER 1941

THE FALLOUT FROM Operation Squatter had not dampened Captain Stirling's enthusiasm – nor his belief that hit-and-run squads operating deep behind enemy lines could prove a vital weapon in the fight against Rommel's resurgent Africa Korps.

To Stirling's mind, the failure of Squatter did not lie in the essentials of the plan ... only in the finer details. The weather undoubtedly played a part – who could legislate for a once-in-a-century storm on the very night of the operation? – but he was smart enough, and humble enough, to understand that future success meant not laying the blame for the fiasco solely on the elements. Almost immediately upon arriving back at base, physically battered, ego bruised, Stirling petitioned for another shot at the German airfields.

Whether Squatter had been bad luck or bad foresight was now irrelevant. This time, he argued, he had a new plan. Unbelievably, he managed to convince General Auchinleck that the SAS was worth another go.

Or perhaps not so unbelievably.

Captain Stirling – or to give him his full due, Captain Archibald David Stirling, son of Brigadier-General Archibald Stirling and grandson of Simon Fraser, 13th Lord Lovat, a descendant of Charles II – was one of the most singular individuals ever to have served in the British armed forces, let alone the SAS. He was also, certainly to modern eyes, very much a product of his time: a dashing, roguish, aristocratic gentleman-soldier, almost a cliché of the classic adventure-book hero.

Born into the Scottish upper classes in 1915, Stirling was raised in the family's ancestral home, the magnificent Keir House estate covering 15,000 acres of Perthshire, and educated at the exclusive Ampleforth College, where he excelled on the sports field, before winning a place at Trinity College, Cambridge. He didn't stay there long – after just one year he was sent down from the university, supposedly for showing more interest in drinking and gambling than his studies.

From Cambridge he departed for Paris with ambitions to become an artist, though he was side-tracked again by an expedition to climb Mount Everest (a decade and a half before Sir Edmund Hillary successfully scaled the mountain). Sadly, or luckily, preparations were cut short by the outbreak of war, and within a year he had volunteered for the new British commando force, shortly after its formation in 1940.

Stirling's highly irregular initial means of presenting his plan for the SAS to high command was typical of the man – maverick but charming, brilliant but unconventional – Trinity College, Cambridge aside, a natural-born winner.

As the remains of L Detachment, Special Air Service Brigade returned exhausted and downcast, Stirling used all of that persuasive charm to explain why the next mission would be a success. Reluctantly convinced, British command gave him one more chance.

Stirling was to head back to the Axis airfields, this time

targeting bases at Tamet and Sirte, on Libya's northern coast. The objective would be the same – materializing apparently out of thin air, the raiders would slip through the light security cordons under the cover of darkness, and once inside, destroy as many aircraft as possible before vanishing into the desert again. The enemy wouldn't know what hit them until it was too late.

The difference this time was that Stirling's force would number only fifteen, and rather than risk another parachute drop, they would drive cross-country with the experienced Long Range Desert Group, who would drop them off (and pick them up again) just 3 miles (5 km) from the target.

On 10 December, Stirling and his men, barely recovered from their previous ordeal, loaded the trucks with bundles of explosives and set off on the punishing three-day drive across the unforgiving Libyan desert.

Travelling by land may have held many advantages over another flight in the heavy, near-obsolete Bristol Bombays, but it was by no means a risk-free, or even straightforward, operation. The Western Desert looked a smooth expanse of sand from the air, but on the ground it was a rocky, jumbled wasteland, broken up by sudden gullies, wadis and ridges. Driving in a straight line for any distance was impossible, and even for the men of the LRDG, who had been operating in these conditions for months, it was tough going.

Under the scorching sun, tyres punctured and burst, the trucks frequently overheated or broke down, and sudden dips and shallows meant regularly digging the heavy vehicles out of the sand by hand – backbreaking work in the best of conditions, but in the Libyan desert, even in December, a Herculean task. At night, not daring to risk a fire so far behind enemy lines, Stirling's men shivered and froze as the temperature plummeted.

In addition, German and Italian planes ruled the skies above North Africa. Twenty-four hours a day, eyes squinted and ears strained for signs of a patrolling fighter or reconnaissance aircraft. There was no respite – from the trials of the desert, or from the threat of the enemy.

For three stop-start days, the trucks rolled north towards the coast until, finally, the drop-off point was reached, and, shouldering their weapons and the heavy packs of explosives, the task force set off on foot. It would not be long before they were spotted.

◆ ◆ ◆

Stirling's team were barely a mile (1.6 km) from Sirte when an Italian fighter plane passed overhead ... before banking, wheeling and heading back, straight for them. As the men dived for the sand, it dropped two bombs. Miraculously, both missed. The commandos grabbed their packs and ran for the nearest cover, camouflaging themselves as best they could in a scrubby, dried-up wadi.

Sure enough, the plane soon returned, along with another two fighters, and for the next ten terrifying minutes, the three aircraft relentlessly strafed the area, chopping up the sand with incessant bursts of gunfire, transforming the desert into a spitting, deadly sea of lead and flying rock.

As the commandos of L Detachment lay motionless in the face of the onslaught, unable to do anything but pray not to catch a bullet and wait for the inferno to end, one of their number seemed untroubled. Robert Blair 'Paddy' Mayne, the man who had come closest to making Squatter some kind of success and Stirling's number two on the mission, spent the attack calmly reading a paperback book.

No casualties were sustained, but Stirling knew that once again his mission was in trouble. After the botched raids on Gazala and Timimi he could not afford another failure – but the news of a British raiding party so close to Sirte surely meant that any element of surprise had been lost. An attack on that airfield was now out of the question.

Splitting his party, he instructed Paddy Mayne to take seven men and most of the explosives and head 15 miles (24 km) west, where they would hit the enemy at Tamet. The two groups would reconvene at the LRDG rendezvous.

◆ ◆ ◆

Lieutenant Paddy Mayne was integral to Stirling's vision of what the SAS should be, and could become. After General Auchinleck had first signed off on his proposal, Mayne was among his very first recruits. Just a few months older than Stirling, the fiery Irishman arrived with a colourful reputation.

A practising barrister in Belfast when war broke out, he was also something of an Irish sporting hero. While studying law at Queen's University he had become Irish heavyweight boxing champion, and later won caps for Ireland and the British and Irish Lions rugby union teams, playing in all three of their tests on the Lions' 1938 tour of South Africa.

It was with the Lions that Mayne's other reputation was forged – as a hard-drinking wild man. Stories from that tour are now the stuff of rugby legend: Mayne smashing up hotel rooms, brawling with dock workers in local pubs, attempting to bust a convict out of jail, and skipping a formal dinner with local dignitaries to go antelope hunting, later dumping the bloody carcass of his night's adventures in the lobby of his hotel.

If war had cut short his sporting and legal careers, it only encouraged Mayne's wild side. Among the first to volunteer for the commandos after its formation in 1940, by the time he came to Stirling's attention, he had already been mentioned in despatches for his bravery in leading a bloody battle against the Vichy French forces in Lebanon. He was also, so the story goes, in jail at the time of his SAS call-up, awaiting court martial for striking a commanding officer after a night's heavy drinking. Just how true that story is remains a subject of debate, but what is beyond doubt is that Mayne's singular mix of brawn, bravery, brains and volatility made him a force to be reckoned with – and, as the airmen at Tamet were about to find out, a fearsome opponent.

On the night of 14 December, Mayne led his men to the edge of the airbase. Stirling had been right about Rommel's misplaced confidence in the power of the desert as an unbreachable defence: there was little or nothing in the way of security surrounding the airfield. Scarcely believing their luck, the commandos slipped through the flimsy perimeters unseen.

Their first target: a large tent that served as the officers' mess. As the British soldiers crept towards it, sounds of laughter and shouting echoed across the base, Italian and German voices, enjoying an evening together, eating, drinking, playing cards, safe in their belief that the enemy was hundreds of miles away.

The merriment was cut abruptly short by the crash of the door shattering under the impact of a heavy boot. Filling the entrance to the tent was the huge figure of Paddy Mayne, bearded and unkempt after days roughing it in the desert, gun held hip-high.

Stunned, the airmen could only stare. What happened next has become part of special forces mythology.

'Good evening,' said Mayne, and opened fire.

What followed was a massacre. Caught by surprise, the German and Italian soldiers were gunned down before they could even reach for their weapons. As the tent erupted into a screaming chaos of blood and bullets, several of the commandos remained in the doorway, still shooting, while Mayne and the rest of the team quickly moved around the airfield, rigging charges to as many planes as they could and smashing up the cockpits of the rest. Other explosives were set to blow fuel and ammunition dumps, as well as a line of telegraph poles.

And then they were gone, as quickly as they came, terrible phantoms in the night. Behind them, fuses detonated, bombs exploded, and Tamet airfield became an inferno. Twenty-four Axis planes were destroyed or fatally damaged in just a few minutes, as well as vital supplies of ammunition, fuel and communication lines.

Paddy Mayne's raiding party also left up to thirty German and Italian soldiers dead, cut down in the officers' mess.

The raid was a stunning success. Not a single British commando was lost. And as if to reinforce just how successful it had been, Mayne returned to Tamet two weeks later on 27 December and, in an almost identical attack, destroyed another twenty-seven planes, as well as three trucks and a supply of spare parts for the aircraft.

Paddy Mayne had shown just how effective Captain Stirling's vision of the SAS could be. Over the next year, copycat operations across the desert would see the force destroy more than 300 aircraft, with Mayne alone accounting for 100 planes taken out of action, a tally higher than that of the top two RAF fighter aces combined.

The raid on Tamet was the beginning of a merciless series of operations for the elite new unit of the British army. If some senior officers – including Captain Stirling himself – privately condemned the killing of the thirty airmen as excessively cruel and against the principles of gentlemanly conduct, Paddy Mayne did not care. Gentlemen be damned. This was war. Who dares wins.

OPERATION ALBUMEN

GERMAN-OCCUPIED CRETE, 7–13 JUNE 1942

BY EARLY SUMMER 1942, Stirling and Mayne's smash-and-burn operations in the desert had given the special forces unit a fearsome reputation. The SAS was barely a year old, but had already more than lived up to expectations – both in the material damage it had caused the enemy and in the psychological war it simultaneously waged.

For so long the Afrika Korps had held the upper hand in the continent. Led by a tactical genius and backed up by superior air power, the German soldiers felt immune from Allied attack.

Wave after wave of SAS operations had put paid to that. Night after night the British commandos struck at airfields and supply depots miles behind enemy lines, appearing like ghosts out of the desert and bringing death and destruction with them. Rommel's men no longer felt secure even in their own bases. Darkness in the desert had become a time of terror, and Stirling himself had acquired a nickname among the frightened German troops: 'Der Phantom Major'.

To British command, the success of these raids had also shown the importance of different special forces units working together, utilizing their unique skill sets to become greater than the sum of their parts. The spectacular raid on Tamet airfield had made the SAS's reputation, but it would not have been possible without the skill, bravery and expertise of the men of the Long Range Desert Group. And it would not be long before the Phantom Major and his band of deadly commandos partnered with another special forces unit with very different talents as they looked beyond Africa.

The Special Boat Service had been formed almost in parallel with the SAS. As David Stirling had been outlining his plans to Allied Command in Egypt, so thousands of miles away in Scotland, another maverick visionary was trying to persuade his superiors of a similarly bold new way of fighting.

Roger Courtney was thirty-seven when war was declared, and immediately volunteered for the commandos, despite having a decade (or in some cases, nearly two decades) on many of the other men. Although trained as a bank clerk, he had quit the straight life – and England – seven years before to become a gold prospector and big-game hunter in Africa. It was while adventuring there in the 1930s that he discovered his other great passion: canoeing. He even paddled the length of the Nile equipped, so the story goes, with only an elephant spear and a sack of potatoes.

Courtney's love of adventure was married to a keen sense of mischief. On a brief visit to Scotland, he used the hoof of a hippopotamus he had brought back as a hunting trophy to make a series of huge footprints on the shores of Loch Ness. The resulting 'proof' of the existence of the Loch Ness Monster became a national sensation before finally being exposed as a hoax.

This combination of fearlessness and devilry was to come together in the formation of the SBS itself. From the very beginning of the war, Courtney had argued for a specialized commando unit using collapsible kayaks to infiltrate enemy positions from the sea. The lightweight canoes were not only silent and so low in the water as to be almost invisible; they were also easily carried, stored and hidden. In skilled hands, a small team of brave men could use the kayaks to slip past defences for reconnaissance and sabotage raids before disappearing out to sea again undetected.

For a man who had canoed the length of the Nile with only a spear and some potatoes to survive on, the idea seemed a no-brainer. For Courtney's superior officers, putting men to sea in such flimsy kayaks seemed reckless at best, and close to insane at worst.

Finally, frustrated at their lack of vision, Courtney took matters into his own hands. While stationed in Scotland, he used the cover of darkness to paddle his canoe up the River Clyde to HMS *Glengyle*, a large infantry landing ship, before climbing the five and a half yards (5 m) up the anchor chain, writing his initials on the door to the captain's cabin, and stealing the cover from a deck gun ... all completely alone, and undetected.

To reinforce his point, he then presented the gun cover to the captain himself, as he attended a meeting with other senior naval officers at a nearby hotel, calmly handing over his prize still dripping wet. Although the *Glengyle*'s captain was not amused, his fellow officers were – and Courtney was promoted to captain and given authorization to form the SBS.

In June 1942, the SAS and SBS would come together for their first significant joint operation – with stunning results.

◆ ◆ ◆

The SAS raids in Libya had proved a vital weapon in the desert war, but even after accounting for the hundreds of aircraft Stirling's men had destroyed, the Luftwaffe still controlled the skies, and – perhaps due in no small measure to the Phantom Major – had transferred their main airbases to the Mediterranean island of Crete, some 200 miles (322 km) north of Tobruk. With all mainland Europe under Axis control, German transport, reconnaissance and bomber planes could operate from Cretan airfields with near impunity, all but safe from Allied attack for hundreds of miles.

Or so they thought.

Operation Albumen aimed to change all that. What was to be the first Allied sabotage mission in occupied Europe targeted Luftwaffe bases at the towns of Kastelli and Heraklion, on Crete's rocky northern coast. Small teams from the SBS and SAS would be transported across the Mediterranean by submarine, before paddling ashore under cover of darkness. The SBS would take out Junkers Ju 88 bombers and Messerschmitt Bf 109 fighter-planes at Kastelli, while the SAS simultaneously sabotaged the larger Heraklion airfield. Both attacks were scheduled for the night of 7 June.

For their part, the SBS operation went according to plan. As Captain Courtney anticipated, the small team of three commandos in their lightweight canoes slipped through the waters unseen by the enemy, and after rendezvousing with four local resistance fighters, infiltrated Kastelli and planted their bombs before the enemy even knew they were there. By the time they had slipped away again, five aircraft had been destroyed and another twenty-nine damaged, as well as vital supplies including a large amount of aviation fuel blown up. All seven saboteurs escaped uninjured.

The SAS had it rougher.

Dropped by submarine just out of range of enemy surveillance, the team of six were led by L Detachment Acting Captain George Jellicoe, along with four commandos from the Free French Forces and Lieutenant Kostis Petrakis from the Greek army. Their plan was to row ashore in three two-man inflatable dinghies, and after landing at Karteros beach just a stone's throw east of the target, stash the boats in the rocky coves, ambush Heraklion at the same time as the SBS men were attacking Kastelli, and, amid the resulting chaos, disappear again into the calm waters of the southern Mediterranean.

Conditions were against them. Battling choppy seas and rising winds, it was all Jellicoe's men could do to keep their heavier dinghies from being blown back out to sea. Whipped by spray and struggling to stay afloat as the boats rose and fell crazily in the surf, their muscles strained and backs bent, they relentlessly dug their oars into the sea, only to be dragged further east with every stroke.

Finally, after hours of gruelling rowing against the wind and tide, the three dinghies finally made land, miraculously still together and with no casualties. Utterly exhausted, the six men used the last of their energy to hide the boats, find cover and collapse into sleep, just as dawn broke.

The morning confirmed Jellicoe's fears. His force had shored at a beach near the tiny village of Malia, blown over 20 miles (32 km) from their target. In one sense they were lucky – had they been another few miles east, where the land dipped sharply south after the headland at Chomatistra, there would have been nothing but hundreds of miles of the Mediterranean before them.

On the other hand, according to the original plan, the mission should have already been over, Heraklion airfield blown, and the raiders safely on their way back to Egypt. Forced to lay up during the day, Jellicoe's men were already twenty-four hours behind schedule, and still had a long and dangerous hike across enemy-occupied terrain before them.

There was never any question of turning back, however, and the commandos broke their temporary camp as the last of the sun's rays dipped below the horizon to the west. For three long, demanding nights they made their tortuous way cross-country, avoiding roads and open ground, scrambling over gullies and rocky scrublands, pushing their way past spiky thorn fields, forcing a path through dense pine forests. A 20-mile (32-km) march through the Cretan wilderness would present a challenge in the best conditions: doing so effectively blindfolded by the coal-black night, hauling equipment that was only intended to be carried a mile or two (1.5 to 3 km) at most, and with senses straining for sight, sound or smell of the enemy, stretched even the toughest of the men to breaking point.

For three nights they marched; for three days they hid, silent, still, hot and hungry. Jellicoe kept morale up with a promise to his men: they were going to make the Germans pay for every minute of this.

Finally, on the night of 12 June, the team reached Heraklion, and from a high position Jellicoe assessed the situation. Once again, luck was against them. The airfield, far from settling down for the evening, was ablaze with light and noise. The commandos had arrived just as the Luftwaffe were embarking on a night-long series of bombing sorties.

It was not lost on the raiders that had the operation gone to plan, no planes would have taken off from Heraklion that night. Every Allied soldier killed or injured by a bomb dropped from one of those Junkers would have been spared. Again, the promise was repeated: the Germans were going to pay.

And then, finally, some good fortune.

The following evening, Jellicoe led his men stealthily down from their hideout, creeping towards the base with guns cocked and packs stuffed with explosives. As they approached, however, a sudden sound shattered the silence. An air-raid siren wailed. Searchlights lit up the sky. There was shouting, men running.

The commandos hit the deck, rifles ready. Had they been spotted? For a long, agonizing few seconds everyone held their breath ... until a new sound, a low, deep droning from the skies directly above, confirmed the real reason for the sudden activity. Those were the sounds of British bombers. Tonight of all nights, the RAF were fighting back.

In a move of astonishing bravery, Jellicoe seized the moment to attack. Even as Allied bombs began falling, he led his men into the heart of the chaos. What German soldiers weren't manning the anti-aircraft defences were already heading for the shelters; nobody thought to guard the airfield from a simultaneous land assault.

With all eyes pointed skywards, the commandos moved through the airfields unnoticed, fast and deadly, exploiting the distraction to get among the Junkers and plant their own explosives. Any soldiers who did spot them were silenced before they could raise the alarm: amid the clamour of bombs and sirens and AA-weapons, their gunfire went unheard.

Before the RAF had finished their raid, the men from the SAS had fled into the mountains again, delayed-action bombs exploding behind them. All six commandos who had landed late and wildly off course in Malia had made it out of Heraklion alive. Behind them lay only destruction.

In addition to the impact of the RAF bombers, at least twenty Junkers Ju 88s were destroyed by Jellicoe's men that night, plus dozens more damaged. Together with the raid on Kastelli, the combined SAS and SBS operation incapacitated an estimated seventy-four planes and blew up over 200 tons of aviation fuel as well as large supplies of explosives and military vehicles. Twelve German soldiers were also killed.

Ten days later, all the SAS men, plus Petrakis, escaped Crete hidden in a fishing boat, after another gruelling hike of 50 miles (80 km) to the village of Trypiti, on the island's southern coast. The four soldiers of the Free French were not so lucky: separated from their SAS colleagues in the mountains, they ran into a German patrol – in the ensuing fight, one was killed and the other three taken prisoner.

Further tragedy befell the Greek resistance. In reprisal for the attacks, the following day the Germans rounded up fifty locals at random, marched them to Heraklion city walls, and executed them in cold blood. Among the victims were lawyers, teachers, farmers, factory workers and even a priest. They are still remembered in Crete today as martyrs.

That atrocity aside, Albumen was a huge victory for the Allies. As well as marking a historic collaboration between two separate branches of British special forces, it had inflicted an important blow to Rommel's supply lines and air support, and, perhaps most significantly, shown the enemy that they were not safe from the Phantom Major, even across the sea in occupied Greece.

The SAS's reach was expanding beyond Africa, and would soon look to strike at the heart of Axis power in mainland Europe.

OPERATION CHESTNUT

SICILY, 12 JULY 1943

AS THE TWO RAF Albemarle transport planes made their way across the Mediterranean, the mood in the back was buoyant. Ten SAS commandos were packed into each of the cramped, draughty aircraft as they rattled over the sea towards Sicily; with them were canisters containing explosives and ammunition, as well as food rations and radio equipment.

It was little wonder spirits were high. Three days earlier, two Allied armies led by General Eisenhower – later to be President Eisenhower – had landed on the Italian island. Fighting was fierce, but significant progress had already been made. A few months before, Rommel had fled back to Berlin, his once-fearsome Afrika Korps finally overrun and defeated.

The tide of war had turned. And now the Allies looked to Europe.

The twin SAS teams packed into the Albemarles were tasked with playing a vital part in Eisenhower's invasion of Sicily. As troops from General Montgomery's British Eighth Army and American forces led by Lieutenant General George S. Patton stormed twenty-six beaches across the southern and eastern coasts of the island, they were to parachute deep inland to carry out sabotage and ambush operations designed to cause havoc behind enemy lines.

After two years of hard fighting, the SAS was now a crucial weapon in the British army, but it had suffered significant setbacks along the way. In early 1943 the force lost its inspirational leader, after Major Stirling was captured by the Germans during a mission in Tunisia. Despite escaping, he was quickly recaptured by Italian troops and eventually sent to Colditz Castle in Germany. He would not see active service for the rest of the war.

In his stead, Paddy Mayne took command of 1st SAS, and a second SAS regiment was formed. It was to be these men who would conduct Operation Chestnut – their first parachute raid into enemy territory.

The plan was to utilize the special forces' expertise at deep cover, infiltration and sabotage to harass and disrupt enemy transport, communication and defences in a series of lightning strikes across the north-east and central areas of the island. The two ten-man units would parachute in under cover of darkness, carry out their missions, and then reconnect with the advancing Allied troops.

The objectives were clear and precise. The first party, led by Captain Philip Pinckney and codenamed 'Pink', was to disable telephone communications in the north-east and destroy the railway connecting the strategically vital ports of Messina and Catania. The second group, led by Captain R. H. Bridgeman-Evans (and codenamed 'Brig') was to infiltrate and destroy the Axis headquarters at Enna, in the centre of the island, and then ambush enemy road convoys heading south to fight the Allies.

The planning was markedly less precise. Initially, the men were to be landed by submarine in the weeks before the invasion for an extended campaign of deep cover disruption and sabotage; that idea was abandoned as too risky at the last minute, and the

12 July parachute drop was hastily arranged instead. It was also decided that the commandos would carry minimal supplies, so as to maximize their speed and stealth, but that a second drop of reinforcements would be made the following day, coordinated by radio with the men on the ground.

Chestnut may have had an air of hastiness and improvisation in its details, but for the twenty SAS soldiers involved, it all seemed simple enough: get on the ground, do what they did best, and relish the chance to give Mussolini a bloody nose ... and in his own backyard, at that. If they could see off Rommel, they could deal with the Italians.

As the featureless black of the sea gave way to beaches and then mountains, Italian air defences lighting up the sky around them, the men were itching to jump.

Finally, the signal came, the heavy doors opened, the supply canisters were pushed out, and one by one, the commandos plunged into the humid Sicilian night.

◆ ◆ ◆

Things went wrong the moment the Pink party hit the ground. Misjudging the drop zone and the wind speed, the men were scattered around the northern slopes of Mount Etna, some 40 miles (64 km) from Messina. By the time they had regrouped they discovered more bad news. Whether through poor packing, poor design, faulty parachutes or simply the volcano's unforgiving rocks, almost all of the canisters containing their food, ammunition and explosives had smashed on impact with the ground. Worse still: every one of the radios was damaged beyond repair.

Without communication, the group had no way of contacting

their base, or the aircraft scheduled to make a supply and reinforcement drop the following night. They were on their own, with no radio, no explosives, minimal rations and barely any ammo, with anything up to 80 miles (129 km) of enemy territory between them and safety.

Captain Pinckney made the difficult call. Mission abandoned. The best they could do now was to try to make their way back to Allied lines.

Brig party fared even worse. While Pink had been blown onto the hard slopes of Mount Etna, Sicily's famous volcano was at least uninhabited. Brig's transport had delivered its party more dangerously off-target. Missing their drop zone by miles, the commandos landed perilously close to the base at Enna, and were immediately spotted.

Fighting from the moment they touched ground, it was all they could do to beat a retreat into the cover of the countryside. Some did not make it, including Captain Bridgeman-Evans himself, who was quickly captured.

For days, the survivors from Pink and Brig parties made their slow, dangerous way south, dodging patrols and hidden enemy defences, fighting where they had to, low on ammo and cut off from radio contact. Little or nothing had been achieved, but in surviving at all, the men of 2nd SAS had once again showed their mettle.

Most eventually made it to friendly lines – thanks in no small part to the swift advances the Allies made through the island – but it had come at a price. As well as the capture of Bridgeman-Evans, another high-ranking officer had been lost, even before things went wrong on the ground. Major Geoffrey Appleyard, former commander of the Small Scale Raiding Force, from which 2nd SAS had been formed, was on board the Pink party transport as drop supervisor, but after making its drop the plane got caught up in anti-aircraft fire and was shot down.

Operation Chestnut failed to achieve any of its objectives, with the official report noting that it had not been worth the 'number of men, amount of equipment and planes used'. The report also observed that 'lessons have been learnt' with respect to the poor planning and hasty changes made in the days before the operation. It would not be long before that claim was put to the test.

OPERATIONS BEGONIA
AND JONQUIL

NORTHERN ITALY, 2–6 OCTOBER 1943

A DANK OCTOBER NIGHT on the eastern Italian coast and in the woods above the beaches, the men from 2nd SAS kept one eye on the road for German patrols, and the other out to sea, scanning the gloom for sight or sound of the expected rescue boats. Rain threatened, the boats were late and as the skies clouded over still further, visibility dropped and the men grew edgy. Despite the tree cover, theirs was an exposed position, trapped between Nazi-occupied northern Italy and the unforgiving waters of the Adriatic.

And then there was the matter of the 600 frightened, starving, exhausted Allied prisoners of war they were guarding. The prisoners – who had escaped from POW camps as Italian troops fled the invading British and American armies from the south – had left the camps with nothing but the clothes on their backs, and after weeks in the wild they were at the limits of their endurance.

The Italians might have capitulated, but Italy was not free, and certainly not safe. The Germans still held a fierce defensive barrier known as the Gustav Line stretching coast to coast some 60 miles (97 km) north of Naples, and they had no intention of letting hundreds of good Allied men return to fight another day.

The SAS's mission was to gather as many of these former POWs as they could and shepherd them to the coast where they could be taken to safety. Over four days, 600 Allied prisoners had been found and brought to the agreed rescue point on the beaches. But now it seemed something had gone wrong.

As the men huddled in the woods and 2nd SAS waited for boats that never came, the night's silence was broken by the sharp crack of a pistol.

The special forces men froze, weapons ready. The prisoners, already terrified, did not. Someone cried out. Someone else made a run for it. The night erupted with shouting German voices, a submachine gun exploded into life, and the former POWs panicked.

◆ ◆ ◆

Begonia and Jonquil were planned as twin rescue operations. After the fall of Sicily, the Allied invasion of Italy had enjoyed spectacular early success, the American Fifth Army and General Montgomery's British Eight Army advancing through the south of the country with ease. Within a few weeks from the initial beach landings on 3 September 1943, the Italians had surrendered, and the Germans pushed back to the Gustav Line, effectively dividing Italy in half.

Sixty-one men from 2nd SAS supported by Eighth Army Airborne would penetrate the area between the towns of Ancona and Pescara on the Adriatic coast. Begonia was the airborne operation – the SAS men parachuting inland on 2 October – and Jonquil was an amphibious landing two days later. Both forces would come together, along with their rescued men, for evacuation by sea, with Allied landing craft supported by requisitioned local fishing vessels.

But just three months after the debacle in Sicily, it seemed the lessons of Operation Chestnut had not been learned. Once again, poor planning and a lack of proper on-the-ground communication were to put the lives of British special forces men at risk.

◆ ◆ ◆

Not all of the mistakes of Begonia–Jonquil were the fault of Allied Command, and strangely, at least one of those mistakes may have saved the operations from being an unmitigated disaster.

Records released after the war show that German intelligence not only knew about the airborne operation, but had even identified the drop points the SAS were to parachute into. As the Allied planes flew inland past Ancona on the night of 2 October, scores of German troops waited for them, hiding in the fields at the drop zone, machine guns ready, poised to pick off the British men one by one as they drifted down through the sky, helpless and horribly exposed, live target practice for the Nazis.

Had Begonia been executed properly, the team would have jumped straight into a trap – and a potential bloodbath.

On the night itself, however, changing weather conditions and inaccurate navigation meant that, once again, the commandos missed their targets. The German troops waited under empty skies, while miles away, the SAS men, initially frustrated at parachuting into the wrong area, met only light resistance after landing.

Melting into the Italian countryside, the Begonia team were able to execute the first part of their operation – to locate and escort the lost, wandering, starving and frightened former prisoners – successfully.

Perhaps too successfully. By the time they reached the coast and the rendezvous with Jonquil, the two forces had between them gathered 600 Allied POWs. All that remained now was to wait for the rescue boats.

Once again, enemy intelligence was one step ahead of them. The Germans had not only known about the Begonia drop zone, they had also intercepted details of the rescue plan. Even as the SAS men and their rescued prisoners made their way to the coast, all of the local fishing boats they planned to use were impounded, and on 5 October, the night before the scheduled extraction, the Germans launched a counter-attack on the Allied-held port of Termoli. As the POWs waited in the woods and the commandos of 2nd SAS scanned the sea for sight of their rescuers, most of the evacuation force were left 80 miles (129 km) south of the rendezvous, fighting their own battles.

Enemy intelligence is one thing, inadequate planning another. Neither the Begonia nor Jonquil team had been issued with radios – so each remained unaware of the developing situation and entirely ignorant of the German attacks on the rescue fleet. Left alone and incommunicado, caught between the enemy and the sea, all they could do was wait, and hope, and wonder what had gone wrong. They had no idea the enemy knew exactly where they were. The shot that had spooked the waiting prisoners was no chance passing patrol, but the first volley of a coordinated attack.

As the Germans advanced on their position and the men from 2nd SAS fought a gritty rearguard action, finally some Allied boats made it to the beaches. For most of the POWs it was too late. Many had fled back into the countryside with the first burst of gunfire; as the fighting intensified, most of the rest followed.

By the time the last SAS commando boarded the rescue vessel and put out to sea, only fifty of the 600 men they had brought to the beaches were evacuated to safety.

What became of the other 550 remains a mystery, and perhaps a tragedy.

OPERATIONS CANDYTUFT
AND SAXIFRAGE

ITALY, 27 OCTOBER 1943

THE SAS WERE NOT done with Ancona and Pescara. The POW rescue operation may have yielded disappointing results, but positives had come from it, and crucially, none of the mistakes made had been the responsibility of the special forces teams. If anything, the actions of 2nd SAS in the face of such obstacles only proved their worth once again.

Operation Begonia had shown that even despite leaked intelligence giving the enemy a head start, the SAS were capable of operating effectively in the region. That only fifty prisoners were ultimately rescued was not the issue: what was important was that the commandos had nonetheless managed to successfully locate twelve times that number, and then escort them safely through enemy territory to the beaches.

And it was not only former POWs that the men of Operation Begonia had gathered during their four days behind the Gustav Line. They returned to base with vital reconnaissance and intelligence information: on German troop numbers and movements, on infrastructure, on supply lines, and on potential new targets.

Just three weeks later, that information would be put to use. The SAS were going back ... and this time they wouldn't be taking prisoners.

The 27th of October 1943 was just two days before a new moon in north-eastern Italy, meaning near-total darkness after 19.00 hours. Low, black clouds had gathered and glowered over the coast all day; finally, around sundown, the heavens opened. It was into these filthy conditions that four teams from 2nd SAS paddled silently and unseen up the Tronto river, midway between Pescara to the south and Ancona to the north, squinting into the driving rain and digging hard against the wind-lashed current. At 22.00 hours they made landfall on the southern bank of the river, stashed and stowed the dinghies, and melted into the countryside to the west.

As with Begonia and Jonquil, the operation was given two separate codenames, but Candytuft and Saxifrage had a common mission. Led by Major Roy Farran and Lieutenant Grant Hibbert, the sixteen commandos were divided into four teams of four. After splitting up into two parties upon landing (so that if one group ran into trouble, the other could continue with the mission undetected), they would make their way inland along the river, before rendezvousing at a strategic junction on the main railway line between Pescara and Ancona. After that ... a return to the SAS's desert roots, and a lightning campaign of chaos and destruction, before vanishing again.

The conditions on the night of 27 October were a mixed blessing. The darkness and relentless rain worked in the commandos' favour in terms of providing cover, but they faced a 5-mile (8-km) hike cross-country in the teeth of the storm before making camp.

Silently, the men hefted packs heavy with explosives, and set off into enemy territory. For most of the night they waded through mud, scrambled through forests and crawled across fields, soaked and whipped by the rain and wind, armed with maps made by the men of Begonia three weeks before and a grim determination to avenge the shortcomings of that mission – and whatever fate had befallen the 550 POWs who didn't make it off the beach.

As dawn brought a lighter grey to the eastern skies but no respite from the deluge, the two parties laid up for the day. Ahead were twelve long, miserable hours lying under cover in cold, wet ditches, taking turns to watch for enemy patrols, trying to catch what sleep they could before darkness fell again, and the real business of the operation began.

Twenty-one hundred hours on 28 October, and the twin raiding parties of Candytuft and Saxifrage met again, exactly on time and on target. Before them, curving gently away to the north and south for as far as they could see in either direction, was the Ancona to Pescara railway, 100 miles (161 km) of vital supply line for the German army.

The saboteurs worked quickly, and in total silence. Explosives were placed, charges were primed, timers were set. Despite the cold and wind and rain and dark, hands remained steady, positions measured and precise. This was what the SAS did; what they were the world's best at doing.

Shortly before midnight it all blew. As the fuses ran down and the charges exploded in sequence, track buckled, sleepers splintered, red-hot rivets flew like bullets into the surrounding countryside. In less than a minute, a large stretch of the railway line had been utterly destroyed. In its place, a crater filled with a mess of twisted steel and broken wood.

Once again, the appalling weather worked in the SAS's favour:

thanks to the howling wind and crashing thunder of the ongoing storm, the explosion went unnoticed by the enemy. The first the Germans knew about it was when the next train derailed, lurching, skidding and crashing off the rails and down the embankment.

By then the sixteen SAS men were long gone. Splitting once more into their two separate parties, they were moving towards the coast again, and their next targets.

◆ ◆ ◆

For the next four days, the British commandos wreaked havoc across the entire region.

Striking at night and using the cover of the continuing storm to move during the day, the SAS men terrorized the coast between Ancona and Pescara in a succession of devastating smash-and-burn raids. Dividing into four independent units meant not only that each of the four-man teams were too fast for the Germans to track, but that they could simultaneously strike at multiple targets miles apart.

In ninety-six destructive hours, the saboteurs blew the railway in no fewer than sixteen separate places, laid deadly mines along several stretches of the coastal road that ran parallel to the tracks, and cut power and communication lines between the two towns.

By the time they reconvened on Halloween night in the valleys west of the town of Salinello, approximately 30 miles (48 km) north of Pescara, almost all transport and communication links between the Germans' two most strategically important Adriatic coast towns had been rendered useless. Two British troopers had been captured, but the fourteen other men were all fully fit and uninjured.

The following night, as the panicked Germans sent

reinforcements north, desperately trying to protect what was left of the railway line, the British commandos stealthily made their way back along the Vomano river to the coast. At midnight they crept to the river mouth and flashed their torches. Once, twice.

The answering signal came immediately. Minutes later, all fourteen were speeding out to sea on a motor torpedo boat, where they would re-join the British Navy and finally, after six days in the storm, covering over a hundred miles (161 km) on foot between them, the men of Operations Candytuft and Saxifrage would be rewarded with a proper cup of hot tea ... and maybe even a bath.

OPERATION TITANIC

NORTHERN FRANCE, 6 JUNE – 17 JULY 1944

THE 6 JUNE 1944 was to be one of the most significant dates in military history – arguably, in human history. D-Day was the largest seaborne invasion ever undertaken: over 150,000 Allied troops stormed a 50-mile (80-km) stretch of the Normandy coast, backed up by an airborne assault by some 24,000 British, Canadian and American paratroopers.

It was also the riskiest Allied play of the war. The fate of all Europe hung on these five beaches: wrest the Normandy coast from the Nazis and all of France would surely follow. Fail to do so, and it could be years before an exhausted, depleted Britain could mount another assault.

Defeat was unthinkable, but victory was by no means assured. That the tide of war had turned was beyond dispute – Allied victories in Africa and the Mediterranean, as well as the failed Nazi invasion of Russia, had put the once-unstoppable German war machine into a defensive standing, forced to consolidate its gains rather than push on to new victories, but that did not mean Hitler was a beaten man.

Far from it. The German army was still a huge, heavily armoured, highly trained and tightly disciplined force to be reckoned with. And, most dangerously of all, Berlin was acutely aware of the Allies' invasion preparations. An operation as vast and complicated as D-Day – or to give it its proper title, Operation Overlord – could not be hidden. The Germans knew the Allies were coming; the only question was where, and when?

For weeks before the landings themselves, another cat-and-mouse conflict raged: one of disinformation, deception, decoy and double-bluff.

The success or failure of Overlord rested almost entirely on the Germans not knowing the precise location of the Allied attack. France's north-west coast bristled with defences as it was – but if Hitler were to intercept Allied plans, he could concentrate his entire force against the exact beaches targeted for the invasion. It wouldn't matter how many hundreds of thousands of men were thrown against them – with the whole might of the German army defending the beaches, the Allies would be slaughtered the moment they touched French soil.

In the run-up to 6 June, British intelligence worked around the clock, turning informants and disseminating false information in an attempt to fool the Germans into thinking the landings would be at Calais, the closest point to Britain, rather than 250 miles (402 km) south, near the Normandy towns of Bayeux, Caen and Sainte-Mère-Église. But still the doubt remained: had Hitler taken the bait? Or would the entire Third Reich be waiting for them?

Finally, in the early hours of the morning of D-Day itself, Allied Command played the last card in its deception campaign. Operation Titanic was to be a dummy invasion, designed to draw German forces away from the beaches of Normandy further inland and to the north.

This dummy invasion was to be carried out by ... actual dummies. Two hundred hessian sacks trussed up to look like

Allied soldiers would be parachuted over drop zones in the countryside near Rouen, 100 miles (161 km) north-east of the real invasion beaches, with another 200 dropped near the town of Saint-Lô, 25 miles (40 km) inland from the American troops at Utah beach.

There was of course one major flaw in the plan. The whole point of this false invasion was that, for as long as possible, it had to look, sound and act like the real thing. Sending actual soldiers on such a mission would be condemning them to almost certain death, but dummies by themselves were not going to fool anyone for very long.

Not for the first or last time, Allied Command looked to the SAS.

◆ ◆ ◆

Intelligence first approached Paddy Mayne. Their proposal: two teams of six men to parachute alongside the dummies and ambush investigating German patrols – partly to prolong the deception of a larger landing force, partly to prevent them from discovering the truth. They would also activate gramophone players loaded with sounds of gunfire and shouting to further spread confusion.

Crucially, the commandos would allow some Germans to escape, in the hope that they would spread the word that hundreds of British paratroopers were landing, and return with reinforcements that would otherwise have been directed towards the invaders on the beach.

Paddy Mayne refused to have anything to do with it. Even the Lion of Africa thought it a suicide mission, and a waste of good men.

Lieutenant Colonel Brian Franks of 2nd SAS disagreed. With a bit of luck and a lot of skill, he believed the right men could not only carry out the operation successfully, but remain hidden long enough for the (real) Allied armies to catch up with them.

Just after midnight on 6 June, twelve SAS commandos and around 400 hessian dummies (affectionately known as 'Ruperts') became the first Allied soldiers to invade occupied France on D-Day.

Led by Lieutenants Norman 'Puddle' Poole and Frederick 'Chick' Fowles, the SAS were dropped with their Ruperts by Halifax transport planes over two zones – one near the towns of Yvetot and Yerville, north of Rouen, and the other in the countryside outside Saint-Lô.

The dummies were more sophisticated than they first appeared. Attached to each were miniature 'noisemakers' – an extraordinary invention for the time, these were portable recordings of gunfire made on magnetic wire – as well as a small explosive charge timed to go off shortly after hitting the ground. The latter were designed to not only destroy evidence that the 'paratrooper' was in fact a Rupert, but also give the impression that he had burned his parachute and disappeared into the countryside.

As Poole and Fowles' men landed in the muddy French fields, gathered up their own parachutes and sought out the canisters containing the gramophone recordings, they scanned the surrounding countryside for signs of the enemy.

To say their feelings were mixed would be an understatement. Under normal circumstances, parachuting deep behind enemy lines at night would mean fervently praying that the drop had not been noticed, that no patrols were on their way to investigate, that their weapons would not be needed just yet.

In this instance, however, they searched the horizon not in dread, but in the hope that German soldiers would appear. The whole raison d'être for the operation was to attract as much attention as possible – and by that reckoning, the more of the enemy they had to fight, Lieutenant Poole grimly observed, the bloody merrier.

As the Ruperts' mini-explosives blew and the hessian paratroopers crackled and burned, the commandos activated the gramophones and, with recordings of shouted orders and gunfire shattering the silence, spread out to wait for whatever the Germans would throw at them.

It did not take long. By 02.00 hours, intercepted communications showed that several German divisions had been diverted to deal with the dummy invasion. Panzer tanks and troops were sent up the Normandy coast from the real invasion beaches to the area around the towns of Lisieux and Le Havre, as well as south to Saint-Lô. It took them until the afternoon to finish searching for the phantom paratroopers, by which time Poole and Fowles' men were long gone, and the Allied landings well underway.

Operation Titanic had succeeded in buying the troops on the beaches a few precious hours' relief from at least one Panzer division, but even despite their efforts, D-Day was not going as well as Allied Command hoped. By the end of the first day, an estimated 10,000 British, American and Canadian soldiers had been killed, and, crucially for the SAS men, the Allies had failed to make significant progress from any of the five beaches. The towns of Bayeux, Caen and Saint-Lô all remained in German hands, meaning the commandos had no way of linking up with friendly forces.

For Lieutenant Poole, this meant a change of plan – and a return to core SAS strategy. For the rest of June and into July, as the men of Operation Overlord struggled their way inland inch by bloody inch, the twelve SAS troopers fought a 'running and gunning' campaign through occupied Normandy, ambushing patrols, sabotaging signal and telephone lines, and working with the French resistance to cause as much havoc as possible until the bulk of the army could catch up with them.

For nearly six weeks they lived on their wits, moving at night and snatching a few hours' sleep during the day, foraging or scrounging what food they could, hunting German patrols and being hunted in turn ... until after forty days, the plan changed again. A local resistance contact reported that three American paratroopers were holed up in a barn some 5 miles (8 km) away. The men had escaped when the lorry in which they were being transported to a prisoner-of-war camp had been strafed by the RAF, and at least one of them was injured.

Lieutenant Poole made the call. He and two other men would make the 10-mile (16-km) round trip across open country that night to bring the paratroopers back to the resistance safe house by first light.

After over a month of criss-crossing the muddy fields of Normandy, sleeping under makeshift cover and dodging enemy patrols and Panzer divisions, the SAS men were almost as familiar with the terrain as locals. Slipping fast and silently through the black night like ghosts, Poole, trooper Anthony Merryweather and another of the commandos made it to the barn in just a few hours.

Once there – and after explaining to the astonished Americans that they were not the vanguard of the Allied armies but in fact a British special forces unit who had been operating undercover in the area since D-Day – Lieutenant Poole assessed the situation. The injured paratrooper was in urgent need of medical attention. Leaving him behind would be tantamount to a death sentence, but taking him with them was equally untenable – there was no question of him keeping up with the saboteurs' running and gunning campaign. Dropping him off with the resistance would only risk all of their lives.

Operation Titanic had enjoyed a long and spectacular run harassing the German army deep in their own territory, but perhaps now it was time to try to return to Allied lines. With Trooper Merryweather carrying the wounded man on his back, they made the 5 miles (8 km) to the safe house before dawn, and prepared to set off west, towards the battle front.

They very nearly made it, too.

◆ ◆ ◆

Against all odds, Poole's team, still carrying the injured American, got as far as no man's land, after a dangerous passage through enemy front lines jittery and on high alert for Allied attack, but, unbeknown to them, their activities over the previous forty days had attracted so much attention that a whole company had been assigned to track them.

Slowed by the injured paratrooper and exhausted and half-starving after six weeks living on little but their nerves, the commandos did not pick up on their hunters until it was too late.

The German troop surprised the SAS men almost in sight

of the Allied lines, ambushing them in open country with a grenade attack. As the ground exploded around them, bodies were thrown or threw themselves into the mud. Some did not move again. Only Lieutenant Poole remained uninjured – and he showed astonishing bravery by making multiple runs under heavy fire to drag his remaining men to the cover of a nearby shelled-out farmhouse.

What was left of the SAS force held out for as long as they could, but eventually, with the house surrounded by at least forty soldiers and more reinforcements on the way, Poole was left with no option but surrender. Just four men remained of the twelve who had landed in the early hours of 6 June; of them, only Poole himself could still stand unaided.

For the SAS, surrender was tantamount to death – literally: according to a directive from Hitler himself known as the *Kommandobefehl* (meaning 'Commando Order'), all special forces commandos captured behind enemy lines were to be executed without trial. Somehow, Poole – pointing to the Americans with them, as well as the fact they were so close to the front line and clearly heading back to Allied lines – convinced his captors that they were not the notorious SAS unit that had caused such chaos for the last six weeks, but in fact simple Parachute regulars separated from their regiment.

The Germans bought it. Trooper Merryweather and two other men were taken to a military hospital in Rennes (and liberated three months later), and Lieutenant Poole was despatched to a POW camp in Germany, where he remained until the end of the war.

In 1945 Poole was awarded the Military Cross for his

skill and bravery during Operation Titanic on the personal recommendation of Paddy Mayne himself. The citation, now held in the National Archives in Kew, concluded: 'Had it not been for this stroke of ill-fortune on the 42nd day of their being within enemy lines, Lt. Poole would have succeeded against overwhelming odds in bringing back his party to the Allied lines. His determination, courage and leadership were of the highest exemplary value and quality.'

OPERATION HOUNDSWORTH

OCCUPIED FRANCE, JUNE–SEPTEMBER 1944

THE WOODLANDS OF the Forêt du Morvan, 1,000 square miles (1,609 sq. km) of forest halfway between Paris and Lyon near the town of Dijon in Burgundy, central France, were ideal territory for a guerrilla army. A vast landscape of thick tree cover over hills, and low mountains studded with villages and smallholdings, all but unchanged for centuries, it remains one of France's most beautiful, unspoilt national parks. In 1944 it was a wilderness.

For three months that summer, this forest was also home to the men of Operation Houndsworth – 18 officers and 126 men of 1st SAS 'A' Squadron, whose activities between 6 June and 6 September proved a vital factor in the success of Operation Overlord, and became a part of British special forces legend.

As Allied troops fought a desperate battle on the beaches of Normandy, 350 miles (563 km) behind enemy lines the SAS were to be engaged in a very different campaign. Their mission: to disrupt and sabotage German supply lines and reinforcements, as well as tie up troops heading for the front – chief among them, the elite 2nd SS Panzer division known as 'Das Reich'. Hardened veterans of the invasions of France and Russia, this formidable tank division numbered over 1,400 vehicles and had been based near Toulouse, on the Mediterranean coast. Stalling their arrival in Normandy was vital to the Allied invasion plans.

The SAS force was led by Major Bill Fraser, one of the original half-dozen officers hand-picked by David Stirling to form the SAS in the desert three years earlier, and, along with Paddy Mayne himself, the last of those still alive and fighting. After leading an initial reconnaissance party parachuted in on the evening of D-Day itself, the main force joined Fraser four days later.

This was to be no 'run and gun' operation – Fraser's men came ready to inflict serious damage, backed up by nine jeeps armed with .303-calibre Vickers 'K' machine guns and two 5-pounder (2.25-kg) mortar anti-tank guns, as well as arms and ammunition for the local resistance groups, known as 'Maquis'. Just in case their intentions were not clear enough, the men wore full uniform and red berets: they were no undercover spies, but a fully fledged squadron of British soldiers, in France to fight a war.

After establishing a base deep in the forest, they made contact with the local Maquis and set about causing havoc.

For three months the SAS men harried and harassed the Germans around Dijon, ambushing patrols, attacking bases, blowing up ammunition and supply depots, laying mines, destroying bridges and communication links, and radioing in RAF air strikes against more than thirty objectives too large to attack themselves.

They also targeted the main railway lines between Lyon and Paris – a vital artery for the Nazi war machine desperate to move as many men and as much artillery north as possible. For weeks the squadron struck again and again with seeming impunity, blowing up the tracks no fewer than twenty-two times and disappearing once more into the forest before the enemy even knew of the latest attack.

During this time, the cooperation of the Maquis was crucial. These men, mostly farmers, labourers and tradesmen who had lived their whole lives in the region and many of whom had families to protect and support, showed extraordinary bravery in helping the British fighters – even the most trivial-seeming act of giving the soldiers food or basic medical care was an effective death sentence if the SS were to hear about it.

The local resistance went deeper than the formalized Maquis units. In one instance, a Maquis man approached a team working to repair a damaged railway after another successful SAS strike.

'How long before the trains are running again?' he asked, under the guise of friendly small talk. The workmen told him, and then suggested that if the saboteurs wanted to do more damage next time, they would be better off targeting a spot a few miles further up the line. As the Maquis operative feigned a polite lack of interest, one of the men produced a stubby pencil and a scrap of paper and carefully drew a map of the exact position in question. A few days later, the line mysteriously blew right where he had pinpointed, and, as predicted, the repairs took far longer to carry out.

On another occasion, the Maquis sent through word that a train carrying a large amount of munitions was due to pass through the town of Cosne on its way to Paris. Three SAS men led by Sergeant Jeff Du Vivier, another veteran of the SAS's adventures in Libya and one of the Originals of Operation Squatter, commandeered bicycles and, each strapping 30 pounds (13.5 kg) of explosives to their backs, raced down the winding country lanes and through two occupied villages in full British uniform, unnoticed by any enemy patrols.

Outside Cosne they stashed the bikes in the woods and laid into the railway, digging away with their bare hands at the ground around the tracks, working flat on their fronts and in total silence: Cosne was a heavily fortified base, and, armed only with their rifles and handguns, the three men would have stood no chance against a German attack.

It took two painstaking hours to lay pressure charges under a fifty-yard stretch of track and they did so with minutes to spare – even as Du Vivier and his men cycled back cross-country, the charges went off behind them, spectacularly derailing the oncoming train. As it crashed, the ammunitions wagon blew; two engines were completely destroyed and ten other wagons derailed, fatally damaging several anti-aircraft guns.

The bicycles were returned to the villagers undamaged and Du Vivier's team disappeared into the forest again.

Major Fraser's most spectacular success came in August, after two months of terrorizing a huge expanse of Burgundy. Another of his officers, Lieutenant Alec Muirhead, was another of the Originals recruited by David Stirling in Libya, and in the ensuing three years he had built a reputation as a master of laying ambushes. Between them, Fraser and Muirhead concocted a plan to destroy a large and strategically vital synthetic oil refinery in the town of Autun, on the south-eastern edge of the forest.

Calling in an air strike was not an option – the refinery was heavily fortified with anti-aircraft guns – and likewise, infiltrating the factory on foot would be impossible, thanks to the large number of German infantrymen stationed there.

Muirhead had a simpler plan. After keeping the plant under observation for twenty-four hours, he led a team with two mortars and jeeps loaded with the heavy Vickers machine guns into a position above Autun and waited until clear moonlight illuminated the target. At exactly 01.30, he gave the order to open fire.

Bomb after bomb arced through the air before smashing into the refinery with devastating accuracy, the high explosives setting the plant ablaze. And still he wasn't done. As the first rounds left the mortars, the jeeps swept down the road towards the factory, machine guns roaring.

'Mortar bombs were plumping most satisfactorily into the factory area at the range of 700 yards [640 m] and dense clouds of steam were seen rising from broken pipes,' he wrote in his report of the attack, as quoted in *SAS Combat Vehicles 1942–91* by Gavin Mortimer.

Then with a roar the 7 Vickers K opened up at 200 yards
[183 m] spraying the whole area with tracer and incendiary.
Each gun pouring two full pans into the rising steam. Then
there was a shrill whistle and the jeeps came roaring back.
Within twenty-five minutes of the first bomb being fired the
whole column was racing back to the hills. Before dawn had
broken the whole force was back in camp, and sleeping in the
shelter of their parachute tents.

The refinery had been completely destroyed; it was still burning three days later.

◆ ◆ ◆

As had happened in Libya, the SAS had become bogeymen to the Germans, a phantom menace liable to strike at any target, any time.

So fearsome was their reputation that the vast expanse of the Forêt du Morvan became an effective no-go area for the German army – like a latter-day Robin Hood, Major Fraser held near-total control of the woods. Search parties were ambushed, convoys sent into the forest to flush them out were eluded. Among them were the famed and feared Das Reich 2nd SS Panzer division: this elite unit spent three weeks hunting in vain for the British force in Burgundy, rather than repelling the invasion 350 miles (563 km) to the west.

Finally, on 20 August, the Germans caught up with them. Word reached radio operator Corporal David Danger through the Maquis that the SS had discovered the location of their camp in the forest and were mobilizing an attack on the squadron. Worse still: the base had been completely surrounded, and the men inside were unaware of the danger.

Alone, Corporal Danger slipped through the German cordon to raise the alarm. When the attack came, the SAS were ready. The hunters became the hunted, a hail of bullets and destruction from the Vickers machine guns and 5-pound (2.25-kg) mortar bombs holding off the attack long enough for Fraser's men to once again disappear into a new base in the forest.

The Nazis' response was, tragically, typical of their terror tactics. As had happened in Crete the year before, if they couldn't strike at the SAS themselves, they would seek brutal retribution from the local civilians. The villages of Dun-les-Places, Montsauche-les-Settons and Planchez all suffered horrific reprisals, with innocent civilians rounded up and murdered.

By 6 September, Houndsworth was declared mission accomplished, when the squadron finally linked up with the advancing US Ninth Army. Over three months and with the loss of just ten men plus another eight wounded, Fraser's men had blown up the Lyon to Paris railway line twenty-two times, destroyed the oil refinery at Autun, inflicted huge damage on German supply, transport and communication infrastructure, called in at least thirty air strikes, tied up the elite 2nd SS Panzer division for three weeks, and killed or wounded no fewer than 220 Germans, as well as capturing another 130 POWs.

It was, by any measure, a brilliant success. Unfortunately, its sister operation, conducted simultaneously 200 miles (322 km) to the west near the town of Poitiers, was to meet a very different fate.

OPERATION BULBASKET

OCCUPIED FRANCE, 6 JUNE – 7 JULY 1944

CAPTAIN JOHN TONKIN moved carefully on his stomach through the thick undergrowth of the Verrières forest, ignoring the cold seeping damp of morning dew through his clothes and trying to resist the urge to jump up and run towards what he knew was an attack on his camp.

Ahead of him, the staccato rattle of gunfire, shouts in German, the thud and crash of mortar bombs. Answering fire came in bursts from the camp itself, but only sporadically and increasingly infrequently. And then it stopped altogether.

There was a moment of silence, as if the whole world had paused. And then the order came, and the German soldiers stormed the base. Tonkin could only watch.

◆ ◆ ◆

The SAS had been a thorn in Hitler's side ever since Paddy Mayne had first kicked in the doors of the officers' mess at Tamet airfield: so much so that as early as 1942 – when Germany was supposedly still winning the war – the Führer issued his infamous *Kommandobefehl*. In flagrant violation of the Geneva Convention, it decreed that any captured SAS men would not be treated as prisoners of war but shot as spies, even if they were wearing full uniform at the time of their capture. In July 1944 that order was to be used to vicious effect.

Operation Bulbasket was a counterpoint and companion to Houndsworth, and designed to mirror that operation in the woods near Poitiers, in western France. Fifty-five men from 1st SAS 'B' Squadron under the command of Captain John Tonkin were parachuted in, along with jeeps armed with Vickers machine guns, and as with Houndsworth, were instructed to work with the local Maquis to disrupt and destroy communication and supply lines, including the strategic Paris to Bordeaux railway line.

The objectives were the same. The outcome would be very different.

◆ ◆ ◆

Things began well enough. Tonkin's advance party had landed on the night of D-Day, with the bulk of his force arriving five days later, along with the jeeps and machine guns. They had made immediate contact with the local Maquis groups, but without the cover provided by a huge forest like the Forêt du Morvan, moved camps every few days. The advantages gained by the increased mobility were undermined by the squadron's reliance on the Maquis for help finding suitable sites. Informants were everywhere – even after three years of brutal German occupation, even when the liberating Allied armies were fighting their way through Normandy.

Like their counterparts in the east, the men of Bulbasket enjoyed spectacular early success. On the very same day that the last of Tonkin's men arrived, a Maquis source revealed to the captain that a Nazi train pulling at least eleven petrol tankers had been seen approximately 35 miles (56 km) north of their current base at the sidings near the town of Châtellerault. According to the source, these were the fuel reserves for a whole Panzer division – destroying them could delay the tanks for weeks.

Tonkin despatched his second-in-command, Lieutenant Tomos Stephens, to investigate. Borrowing a bicycle, Stephens made the dangerous journey around the heavily garrisoned Poitiers dressed in full uniform, cycling the 70-mile (113-km) round trip and returning later that night to confirm the intelligence correct, but also that the train was guarded by more men than the SAS team could handle.

Tonkin radioed England, and that night a squadron of twelve Mosquito fighter-bombers swooped on the depot at Châtellerault. The train – and its precious cargo of petrol – was obliterated.

For the next two weeks, the SAS men targeted train lines and communication links in fast, mobile raids, moving camp regularly and avoiding open confrontation with the enemy patrols now on high alert for the British commando force. Along the way they also rescued an American airman, Second Lieutenant Lincoln Bundy, who had been hiding out in the area after being shot down.

But by 1 July, Tonkin had begun to feel uneasy. The team had remained in the same camp, in the Verrières forest south-east of Poitiers, for a week, and he felt the Maquis were becoming a little too comfortable with their presence, so much so that girls from the local village had even begun coming to the camp to dance to music the radio operators could pick up from England.

Their presence had become an open secret; it was time to move on.

That night, the SAS men struck camp and, under cover of darkness and without informing the Maquis that they were leaving, headed for a new base, at Bois des Cartes, a few miles to the south-west.

Just a few hours later, they were back. The well at Bois des Cartes had dried up, and without water the site was useless. Tonkin changed plans again: ordering the main force to remain at Verrières under the command of Lieutenant Stephens, he took two men and set off again to scout a new camp.

Captain Tonkin would not see Tomos Stephens, or most of his men, ever again.

Even as he and his companions left that night, a troop of SS soldiers were silently moving through the woods to surround the base. Somebody had betrayed the unit.

Was it a German spy who had infiltrated the Maquis? A villager jealous of the attention the local girls were giving the British men? One of the girls themselves? Or simply someone for whom the lure of Nazi blood money was too much to resist? The identity of the informant has never been found, but the effect of their actions was devastating.

The SS attacked at dawn. Tonkin and his two scouts were on the edge of the woods when they heard the first mortars explode. Dropping to the ground, they crawled as fast as they could towards the fighting, praying that the men inside the base had managed to get out in time.

They had not. As the Germans started their bombardment, most were still asleep. Scrambling for their weapons they returned fire as best they could – and for the whole morning of 3 July, they mounted a brave and desperate defence of the camp, even as Captain Tonkin moved around the edge of the encirclement, doing what damage he could to the attackers.

Surrounded, outnumbered and outgunned, the SAS could not hold out for ever. Eventually, after battling until 14.00 hours and down to the last of their ammunition, Lieutenant Stephens initiated a final escape attempt, leading thirty-three of his men into the woods in a last-gasp bid to outrun the enemy.

They were immediately surrounded, and seeing the futility of the situation, Stephens gave the order to surrender. It was to be his final action – as his men laid down their weapons, an SS officer beat Stephens to death with the butt of his rifle.

If the murder of the unarmed Stephens was horrific, worse was to come. Four days later, the remaining thirty men, including the American pilot Lincoln Bundy, were led back into the woods, forced to dig three shallow pits, and then gunned down in cold blood. Three other SAS troopers, who had been taken to hospital after the attack, were despatched by lethal injection. Hitler's *Kommandobefehl* not only included those who had surrendered, but even extended to men too weak to fight.

In all, forty-four SAS men died on Operation Bulbasket, as well as Second Lieutenant Bundy and at least seven members of the French resistance. Thirty-three of those SAS troopers had been murdered after surrendering. When their bodies were discovered a year later, all apart from Lincoln Bundy were still wearing their Allied uniforms.

OPERATION GAFF

OCCUPIED FRANCE, 25 JULY 1944

THE SPITFIRE OF the Royal Canadian Air Force 412 Squadron wheeled, banked, and then, with the July sun blinding its approach, dived hard and fast, its target a lone car speeding east along the road from Caen to Paris. With no hope of outstripping the plane, the driver threw his vehicle into a desperate series of swerves and skids, veering from one side of the road to the other as his passenger crouched for cover in the back.

He didn't stand a chance. Screaming in low, the pilot thumbed the trigger; machine guns blazed and the road erupted. Deadly parallel lines of bullets raced towards and then around and finally into the car, spitting and tearing, slicing through wood and metal and, eventually, flesh; as the driver's left arm shattered and pulped, he wrenched the wheel in one final manoeuvre, sheering off the road, the vehicle jerking and bouncing crazily across the muddy fields in a last-ditch attempt to make for the cover of the trees before the Spitfire returned for another pass.

The driver had no idea if his passenger was still alive, but his orders were clear: to protect him at all costs. Even as his eyes blurred and darkened and the pain overwhelmed him, he used the last of his strength to jam his foot on the accelerator.

From above, the Spitfire pilot watched as the car smashed into the trees at full speed. Satisfied, he pulled up, turned again, and headed west, back towards England.

The pilot noted the date: 17 July 1944, another kill. It was only one car, but it was a German car, and every German counted.

◆ ◆ ◆

The deception campaign that began months before D-Day and continued through the heroics of operations Titanic, Houndsworth and Bulbasket had bought the Allies an invaluable head start in the liberation of France, but as the Germans regrouped, reorganized and finally mobilized the full power of their forces in Normandy, the fate of Operation Overlord still hung in the balance. And one thing – or rather, one man – worried the Allied commanders above all else.

Field Marshal Erwin Rommel had been given charge of the defence of France as early as November 1943, when it became clear to Hitler that an attempted retaking of mainland Europe was inevitable. The so-called 'Desert Fox', who had very nearly routed the Allies in North Africa, was still the Nazis' most formidable – and most able – commander.

Rommel had long argued that the war would be won or lost on the beaches of northern France and had urged Hitler to concentrate everything he had at repelling the Allies before they could establish any kind of progress into the country. Fortunately, his arguments, at least initially, fell on deaf ears, but nevertheless, with Overlord progressing slower than planned, and Rommel finally being listened to, the experience and tactical cunning of the Desert Fox had become a major concern – not to mention the effect his magnetic charisma and aura of invincibility had on the enemy's morale.

Even Winston Churchill acknowledged the fearsome abilities of the man, telling the House of Commons in January of 1942: 'We have a very daring and skilful opponent against us, and, may I say across the havoc of war, a great general.'

Something had to be done about Erwin Rommel. Once again, Allied Command looked to the SAS to do its dirtiest work.

The men of the Special Air Service and the German field marshal had history. It was largely down to Rommel's sweeping victories in the desert that the SAS had been formed in the first place, and it was in no small part due to David Stirling and Paddy Mayne's trail of destruction across Rommel's Libyan airfields that the Allies finally managed to turn the tide of that campaign.

If there was some level of mutual respect between them, there was also a deadly rivalry. It was time for that rivalry to be resolved, once and for all.

On 20 July, the following top-secret operational orders – revealed in *The SAS War Diary 1941–45*, published by the SAS Regimental Association in 2011 – were issued.

INTENTION: To kill, or kidnap and remove to England, Field Marshal ROMMEL, or any senior members of his staff.

METHOD: The following points should be borne in mind: If it should prove possible to kidnap ROMMEL and bring him to this country the propaganda value would be immense and the inevitable retaliation against the local inhabitants might be mitigated or avoided. Such a plan would involve finding and being prepared to hold for a short time if necessary, a suitable landing ground.

To kill ROMMEL would obviously be easier than to kidnap him and it is preferable to ensure the former rather than to attempt and fail in the latter. Kidnapping would require successful two-way W/T communication and therefore a larger party, while killing could be reported by pigeon.

Six SAS men would parachute into northern France, infiltrate Rommel's fortress headquarters at the Château de La Roche-Guyon, an imposing twelfth-century castle built into a hillside 40 miles (64 km) to the west of Paris, and, by whatever means they deemed necessary, attempt to kidnap the Desert Fox. If they couldn't do that, they were to kill him.

The hit squad was led by French-born Captain Jack William Raymond Lee. Originally christened Raymond Couraud, the twenty-four-year-old had joined the French Foreign Legion as a teenager shortly before the war, before becoming part of the resistance after the fall of France, helping smuggle more than 2,000 refugees to Spain and North Africa. Eventually arrested, he escaped to England, and in 1941 joined the Free French Forces, and two years later, with a change of name and British citizenship, the SAS.

Captain Lee also had a nickname: 'Killer'. He didn't relish trying to kidnap the field marshal, but he had no qualms about assassinating him.

On the night of Tuesday 25 July, Lee and his men parachuted into the countryside near the town of Rambouillet, south-west of Paris and around 40 miles (64 km) south of the Château de La Roche-Guyon. After laying up for most of Wednesday, the assassination squad began moving north at sundown on Thursday.

Moving only at night and avoiding roads and open country, Lee estimated that it would take his team another five days to reach the chateau. But within twenty-four hours everything would change.

On Friday 28 July, new intelligence reached the team. In his official report, also preserved by the SAS Regimental Association, Captain Lee recorded it with what in his mother tongue might be called insouciance.

'Learned that Rommel had been got.'

◆ ◆ ◆

Eight days before the SAS team had landed in France, and a full three days before the 'Kill Rommel' order had even been issued, the field marshal had been in a car crash on his way back from visiting the front lines near Caen. After swerving off the road and hitting a tree, his driver had been killed, while Rommel himself had been thrown clear of the vehicle, suffering three separate skull fractures, as well as multiple facial lacerations. He would be in a coma for five days, before being transferred first to hospital in Paris, and then to his family's home in Ulm, Germany.

The 'only one car' strafed by the lone Spitfire of 412 Squadron on 17 July was Field Marshal Erwin Rommel's car. The 'every German counts' in this particular instance actually referred to the one German Allied Command considered the most dangerous of all.

(Interestingly, and perhaps understandably, credit for the attack on Rommel's car was later claimed by a separate squadron of RAF Typhoons, as well as by the US Air Force, who maintained it was one of their P-47 Thunderbolt pilots who shot the field marshal off the road. If that wasn't confusing enough, there seems to be no explanation as to why it took over a week and a half for intelligence to report that Rommel was injured at all, by which time Captain Lee's hit squad was already deep behind enemy lines, poised to attack a heavily guarded chateau, apparently in vain.)

Either way, Lee's mission was now redundant. And so he did what SAS men do: he adapted.

In a highly precarious position on the western outskirts of Paris, he at first considered an assault on the chateau anyway, before abandoning the idea as unnecessarily risky. Instead, he directed his men to make their way south, and the advancing American lines. They would take their time, and cause as much trouble as possible along the way.

Over the following two weeks, the commandos covered over 100 miles (161 km) of enemy terrain in a trademark 'run and gun' campaign, moving by night and hiding by day, skirting Paris to the west and blowing the train line between Paris and Chartres at least twice along the way. They also set up roadblock ambushes, successfully destroying seven lorries filled with vital ammunition and fuel supplies meant for the front.

In a separate incident, the six men laid an ambush for what they thought would be another lorry convoy, only for a staff car with motorcycle outriders to trigger the trap. In the ensuing firefight, all of the Germans were killed, but as Lee moved in to identify the officer, a further convoy roared down the road, guns firing. The SAS men fled back into the woods, and Lee later noted the officer only as 'certainly a colonel, possibly a minor general'.

Captain Lee's team finally reached the Americans at the town of Brou, south-west of Chartres, on 12 August. The unit had once again shown the skill and determination of the SAS: over nineteen days of dangerous on-the-ground operations in which several dozen enemy soldiers had been killed, they did not pick up a single injury between them, save for a minor bout of food poisoning sustained by Lee himself shortly after landing.

But that is not the end of the story. There remains one more ironic twist to the Operation Gaff tale … and a coincidence of timing that almost defies belief.

◆ ◆ ◆

Allied Command may have considered Erwin Rommel the most dangerous German alive, but he was not the most powerful German in the war. And in July 1944, the field marshal was a crucial factor in a plot that could have dramatically changed the war – and history itself – for ever.

On 20 July, the very same day that Operation Gaff's 'Kill Rommel' order was issued, another assassination plot was reaching its climax. Shortly after noon on that day, Colonel Claus von Stauffenberg, a hero of the Nazi invasions of Poland and Russia, walked into a meeting at Adolf Hitler's Wolf's Lair headquarters carrying a briefcase containing a bomb. Part of a group of high-ranking conspirators known as 'Valkyrie', their aim was to kill Hitler, replace him with a saner leader, disband the Nazi party altogether, and sue for peace with the Allies.

And the conspirators' favoured candidate for this new, more moderate, peace-seeking Reich President? Field Marshal Erwin Rommel.

Hitler escaped the explosion, but only just, and for hours it was reported that the Führer was dead. As confusion and uncertainty gripped Berlin, a man like Rommel might have seized the moment to take charge, and change the war. As it was, and thanks to a chance sighting by a lucky Spitfire pilot three days before, the field marshal was unconscious in a hospital bed at the time.

Rommel survived his car crash, and he survived Operation Gaff's SAS hit squad. But he would not survive the wrath of the Führer. On 27 September, a memorandum was presented to Hitler that claimed 'defendants have testified that Field Marshal Rommel was perfectly in the picture about the assassination plan and had promised to be at the disposal of the New Government'.

On 14 October 1944, Germany's most dangerous general was offered a choice: face trial for treason, or commit suicide. He chose cyanide, and died wearing his full Afrika Korps uniform.

OPERATIONS WALLACE AND HARDY

OCCUPIED FRANCE, AUGUST–SEPTEMBER 1944

IN AN ABANDONED barn on the edges of the Forêt de Châtillon, the toasts came thick and fast – in French, in English, in an improvised mix of both languages. To France! To de Gaulle! To England, the King, God, and Saint George! To the brave men of the Maquis resistance! To the fighters of the SAS! To glory! To revenge! To victory!

Mugs of robust local Burgundy wine were drained and then refilled, again and again, and as the toasts gave way to singing, two men detached themselves from the party and found a quieter spot in the corner. Major Roy Farran of 2nd SAS had a plan he wanted to discuss with the leader of the Maquis. As they spread a map on the floor and Farran began talking – pointing out landmarks, cover, enemy positions, pinch points – the Frenchman grinned.

'*C'est un plan fou,*' he said, '*mais j'aime ça.*'

It's a crazy plan, but I like it.

Behind them, the revelries continued, though each of the SAS men took care not to overdo it. The bombed-out farmhouse in the forest was a secure enough base – and sentries hidden in the woods would raise any alarm long before the enemy even knew they had been spotted – but they were nevertheless hundreds of miles behind German lines. It wouldn't do for a chap to lose his head completely.

The Maquis were not so restrained. After all – they had a lot to celebrate. Since Major Farran's men had arrived they had enjoyed spectacular success against an enemy that had ruled the region with an iron fist since the invasion four years before. And now, fighting with the SAS, and with the British and American armies marching ever closer from the south and west, they felt invincible. As the late August evening gave way to night and the last of the wine was emptied, the cry was raised again: '*Gloire! Vengeance! La victoire!*'

Major Farran raised his own cup and smiled. It was indeed a crazy plan. But then aren't all the best plans a little bit crazy?

◆ ◆ ◆

Operations Wallace and Hardy were, on paper at least, another part of the SAS campaign of harassment and disruption in central France after D-Day. In practice, they became something different altogether.

Hardy was the initial parachuting of a squad of commandos on 27 July into the Forêt de Châtillon, 50 miles (80 km) north of Dijon and approximately 130 miles (209 km) from France's eastern border. Under the command of Captain Grant Hibbert, the veteran of Operations Candytuft and Saxifrage, their job was supposed to be strictly one of contact and reconnaissance. Naturally, Hibbert conveniently forgot the 'strictly' part, and as well as establishing a base in the forest, successfully linking up with the local resistance and scouting out enemy positions, supply lines and movements, he also took the opportunity to create a bit of mischief.

For a month the men of Hardy carried out a series of small-scale lightning strikes, targeting German patrols, mining roads, destroying communication lines, and blowing up a stretch of railway between Dijon and Langres, always attacking at night, always taking care to cover their tracks.

On 27 August they were joined by Operation Wallace, and the real business began.

Wallace was a force of sixty SAS men and twenty jeeps fitted with Vickers machine guns and led by Major Roy Farran, the officer whose activities with Hibbert in the Italian countryside between Pescara and Ancona had caused the Germans such a headache the previous autumn. Rather than parachute into the area, they were instead landed at the Allied-controlled Rennes airfield in Brittany on 19 August, and then drove the 300 miles (483 km) east, deep into German-controlled France.

It was hardly a stealthy approach. Sixty men in twenty jeeps are always going to attract a bit of attention, and Major Farran made sure that, even so far behind enemy lines, their presence was very obvious. In one incident they engaged a full company of infantrymen on their way to the western front, and despite being outnumbered and outgunned, inflicted dozens of casualties without loss; in another they attacked a German radar station with such ferocity the entire garrison guarding it fled.

Just days before linking up with Hibbert's men in the Forêt de Châtillon, Farran led another assault, this time on a train full of troops. Abandoning any subtlety, he ordered the jeeps to fire directly on the engine as it sped down the track – and as round after round from the heavy Vickers machine guns shredded the metal, the train screeched to a halt and the German soldiers poured out. They too were cut down ruthlessly.

The reasoning behind Farran's very noisy passage through

France was deliberate. Unlike previous post-D-Day missions behind enemy lines, Wallace and Hardy were not to be small raiding parties, but a major operation targeting heavily fortified positions in open combat.

The reason? Other than the chaos and damage such activities would cause, the aim was to convince the enemy that the Allied front line was far closer than the enemy thought – and even that Farran's jeeps were actually the advance elements of the US Third Army itself. The SAS were no longer trying to keep the Germans from moving units and artillery westwards towards the front, but were harrying their escape to the east, and the German border. Cause enough chaos, make enough noise, and they might just break ranks altogether.

Farran's adventures hadn't come without loss, however. By the time he reached the forest and rendezvoused with the troopers of Operation Hardy, the squad had sustained eight casualties and were down by thirteen jeeps, but with their combined teams soon reinforced by further RAF supply drops, and a relocation to a new base deeper in the forest, the SAS men were keen to get properly to work.

Over the following three weeks, the united force – now back up to sixty men, led by Major Farran with Captain Hibbert as his second-in-command – stepped up their campaign of havoc, using the speed and mobility of their jeeps to surprise German patrols and fuel convoys in a series of surprise aggressive attacks. On one occasion an ambush killed a German battalion commander; on another, twenty men lay in wait for a convoy of fuel tankers heading for the Panzer division based in Dijon. After allowing the outriders and a lorry full of infantrymen past, the commandos emptied their guns into the petrol tankers themselves. As all five trucks exploded and the entire road was engulfed in flames, the SAS men slipped away before the German soldiers had time to regroup.

Successful though these attacks were, Farran was still not satisfied. He had his eye on a bigger prize – and an assault more daring than anything the squad had yet attempted. But for it to work, he needed the Maquis.

◆ ◆ ◆

The morning before the celebration with the Maquis, Farran and Hibbert had taken a trip to the town of Châtillon-sur-Seine. The ancient city stood on the western edge of the forest, and was the main German headquarters for the area. One hundred and fifty enemy troops were garrisoned there in the magnificent Château du Maréchal Marmont, an imposing seventeenth-century building that dominated the skyline, built on a low hill and surrounded by a wide expanse of grass. Crucially, intelligence had reported that the garrison was due to be replaced within a few days.

With typical bravado, the two men, dressed in full uniform, zoomed through the town in their jeep and parked up underneath the chateau's outer perimeter. Farran gave Hibbert a leg-up and the British captain stood on the wall and calmly surveyed the area.

It was only a minute or two before he was spotted. As the shout went up and guards came running, he calmly vaulted back down and the pair sped off again towards the forest. Nevertheless, it was enough. By the evening Farran had a plan.

Using the inevitable disarray that would come with the

handover of one set of troops for another, the SAS would mount a full-scale attack on the chateau itself. Sixty commandos and their ten remaining jeeps would be supported by 500 Maquis fighters in the operation's most outrageous and audacious manoeuvre to date. What could possibly go wrong?

Only one thing did go wrong, as it turned out.

On the morning of the attack, as the SAS men waited at the agreed rendezvous point, the Maquis were nowhere to be seen. Five hundred resistance men had been promised; but as a pre-dawn grey mist drifted over the Burgundy hills, not a single one showed up.

Farran made a decision. He was resolved to go ahead anyway.

As Châtillon slept, the SAS moved in. Jeeps were placed at roadblocks on strategic junctions approaching the enemy base, Vickers guns primed and ready for the German relief convoy, while the bulk of the men sneaked into the grounds of the chateau itself. Mortars were placed, Bren guns readied.

At 07.00 hours precisely, they opened up with everything they had. Volley after volley of 10-pounder (4.5-kg) shells slammed into the chateau, smashing the walls, a sudden, violent barrage of destruction ripping the building apart. Masonry crumbled, windows smashed, brickwork and stonework collapsed, and as the German troops came running out, the commandos opened fire with their machine guns, cutting them down in a volley of bullets.

The first wave of defenders didn't stand a chance, but the next got wise. Rather than blindly running out of the building, the Germans regrouped, kept under cover and began returning fire. At the same time, Farran got word from the roadblock – the relief garrison was approaching, thirty trucks loaded with fresh men and weaponry.

The odds were changing: sixty SAS troopers with the element of surprise against 150 Germans didn't seem so bad – sixty against 300, half of which were arriving with new ammunition and ordnance, was a different matter.

The jeeps were ready for them, however. As the convoy rolled towards their roadblock, they unleashed their Vickers into the lead trucks – which just so happened to be packed with ammunition. Farran later remembered the scene, as told in *SAS: The Autobiography*, by Jon E. Lewis: 'The first five trucks, two of which were loaded up with ammunition, were brewed up and we were treated to a glorious display of fireworks.'

The battle now raged on two fronts, and as had happened with the garrison in the chateau, the German soldiers in the convoy had recovered from their initial shock and were beginning to reorganize themselves. The danger for Farran was that a significant breakout from either of the positions could see the SAS men trapped in a pincer movement between them. At 09.00 hours, he gave the order to withdraw.

And then something completely unexpected happened. As the SAS broke off and retreated back towards the forest, the Maquis resistance men finally showed up. They weren't the 500 promised, and they were at least two hours late, but nevertheless, they were here now. Farran's sixty men were now over 160, and the odds had dramatically swung again.

The major changed his plan once more. Splitting the combined force in two, he led half the men west, with Captain Hibbert taking the rest east. For a further six hours the two units harried and harassed the Germans from both sides, striking and moving in a constant and chaotic series of attacks that left the enemy thinking that the whole town was surrounded by a far larger force.

Finally, at a little before 15.00 hours, and after fully eight hours of fierce fighting, running desperately low on ammunition and all out of mortar shells, Farran ordered his men to fall back. The Maquis melted back into the countryside; the SAS disappeared into the forest – and the Germans were left wondering what the hell had just happened. The final tally for the battle was over 100 enemy soldiers dead and many more wounded, as well as nine trucks, four cars and a motorcycle blown up ... all for the loss of a single SAS man, plus two more wounded.

Perhaps most importantly, Farran's key deception had worked: convinced that the SAS attack was the advance party of a greater Allied force, the German commander gave the order to withdraw from Châtillon-sur-Seine, weeks ahead of schedule.

The 'crazy plan' had been a stunning success.

◆ ◆ ◆

Major Farran and his men remained in the Forêt de Châtillon for a further two weeks after the battle, resuming their campaign of disruption and destruction, and concentrating especially on an area due east of the forest known as the Belfort Gap, where the borders of France, Switzerland and Germany met, and the quickest way back to the Fatherland for the retreating enemy forces.

By the time they were finally relieved by the (real) advancing US Third Army, the men of Operations Wallace and Hardy had been responsible for more than 500 German casualties and the destruction of at least fifty-nine enemy vehicles, including trucks, petrol tankers, troop carriers and staff cars. They had also blown up a goods train and destroyed over 100,000 tons of petrol – at that stage of the war, a commodity almost as precious as soldiers themselves.

Over the month-long campaign, the SAS sustained just seventeen casualties, including seven dead. Major Farran was awarded a Distinguished Service Order for his bravery and leadership in the operation.

His official report concluded with a sentence that echoed the original ideals of David Stirling himself: 'This operation proves that with correct timing and in suitable country, with or without the active help of the local population, a small specially trained force can achieve results out of all proportion to its numbers.'

OPERATION LOYTON

OCCUPIED FRANCE, AUGUST–OCTOBER 1944

BY THE AUTUMN of 1944, the SAS were the most feared weapon in the Allies' armoury, but with that reputation came a deadly kickback. As Operation Bulbasket had shown, Hitler's Kommandobefehl order was no idle threat: as far as the German army was concerned, the SAS existed beyond the boundaries of conventional warfare. And neutralizing their operations – by whatever means necessary – became priority number one.

Tragically, the murders of thirty-three surrendered men during Bulbasket was not to be the only atrocity committed by the Nazis against SAS troopers in the closing stages of the war. Even as the German army retreated from France to a last-gasp defence at the Rhine, they were still capable of acts of astonishing brutality. In the case of Operation Loyton, the tragedy was made still worse by the failures of Allied Command to properly plan for the situation they were about to put their men into.

Like Operations Wallace and Hardy, Loyton was intended as a means of disrupting the Nazis' retreat to the German border. A small lead party parachuted into the mountainous Vosges region of Alsace, north-eastern France, on 12 August, followed by the main force, led by Lieutenant Colonel Brian Franks, eighteen days later.

Franks was the man who had given the go-ahead for Operation

Titanic, in which the SAS had performed heroics against the odds distracting and decoying the Germans in the weeks after D-Day: he believed his team could do the same now, on the other side of France.

The landing zone was a clearing in the thick forests that covered the mountains, just 40 miles (64 km) west of the German border near Strasbourg. The wild, rugged terrain appeared ideal for a small, mobile attack force; with a base set up in the near-impenetrable woods and with Maquis contacts in the few isolated villages and smallholdings in the area, the plan was textbook SAS – hit the enemy hard, disappear, then hit them hard again somewhere else, always moving, always unexpected, always just out of reach.

With the US Third Army powering eastwards towards Strasbourg, Operation Loyton would act as a kind of advance interference force, sowing chaos and confusion in the demoralized German lines, until being relieved by the advancing Allies.

Unfortunately, it didn't turn out that way. Once again, the men of the SAS would be let down by factors beyond their control: poor communication, and fatally flawed intelligence.

Vosges was not as lightly defended as Allied High Command believed; nor was it as friendly. And there was no sign of the Americans.

◆ ◆ ◆

If Lieutenant Colonel Brian Franks was a superstitious man, he might have had a bad feeling about the operation from the moment his squad touched down. Within minutes of landing in the mountains, things began to go wrong: some frustrating, some almost comical, some tragic.

First, the parachute bearing one of the supply canisters dropped with the men failed to open properly – the heavy container was filled with ammunition and explosives and as it smashed into the ground it burst open and then exploded. That no one was injured was a miracle, but that notwithstanding, the loss of so much vital munitions was a heavy blow.

The next mishap was altogether more surreal. As another of the canisters landed, it was seized upon by an eager member of the local Maquis assisting the drop. Was he hungry? Was he confused? Drunk? Or just stupid? Either way, he did something catastrophic. Without waiting for any of the British soldiers, he opened the canister, reached inside and pulled out what he assumed to be a piece of ... exotic cheese?

Taking cheese to Alsace is roughly equivalent to 'taking coals to Newcastle'. It's something nobody does, least of all a British special forces unit parachuting behind enemy lines for an undercover sabotage operation. Nevertheless, the man took a large bite ... and promptly doubled over in acute pain, poisoned by the plastic explosive now eating its way through his gut. There was nothing the medics could do for him, and he died the same night.

The hapless (and hungry) resistance man was not the only fatality that greeted Franks' arrival. Another Frenchman was apprehended in the drop zone claiming to be innocently picking mushrooms by moonlight. In the resulting confusion he made a grab for a machine gun – and was shot on the spot.

Two local men dead, plus a cache of explosives destroyed: it was an ominous start to the mission. But there were other, less farcical and far more dangerous, factors in play that were to prove even more disastrous.

Unbeknown to Lieutenant Colonel Franks – or, presumably, to the intelligence upon which the success or failure of his whole operation rested – the German army was not in abject retreat in Vosges, but rather rallying for a determined stand against the Allies in the mountains and forests west of the Rhine. The 17th SS Panzergrenadier Division – a mechanized infantry unit hardened by months of battle against the Allies in Normandy – had been assigned to the area specifically to repel the US Third Army advance to Strasbourg. They were itching for a scrap, but, until the SAS arrived, they had no one to fight against.

If Allied intelligence was ignorant of the Panzergrenadier division patrolling the area near Strasbourg, they were also wrong about the progress of the US Third Army. The Americans had indeed powered their way eastwards towards the German border, but they had done so too fast, and too far. By the time they reached the western edge of Alsace they had outrun their supply lines. At the town of Nancy, 50 miles (80 km) west of the SAS force, the American advance stalled, and then stopped altogether. They would not move any further east until after Operation Loyton was concluded.

Franks' men were not to know this, however, and, with another parachute drop supplying them with jeeps and replenishing their lost ammunition, they established a base near the tiny village of Moussey and set about causing trouble.

At first, they were successful: following Major Bill Fraser's 'Robin Hood' model from Operation Houndsworth in the forests 250 miles (402 km) south-west, Franks and his second-in-command Captain Henry Druce used the cover of the thick woods to launch an aggressive campaign against any and all

German soldiers in the area.

Patrols on the winding mountain roads were ambushed, supply and reinforcement lines into Strasbourg from the west effectively cut off by the commandos. Attacks could come from anywhere, the British men swooping out of the forest, shooting and burning and blowing up what they could, before disappearing into the trees again.

By mid-September, and with no sign of the Americans, Franks decided to up the ante, increasing the frequency and aggression of his attacks – most spectacularly, when a force led by Captain Druce roared into Moussey in their jeeps and opened fire on a whole unit of Waffen SS as they formed up in the town square.

A spectacular success it may have been – but Druce's attack would also prove to be a big part of the operation's undoing. Enraged, Erich Isselhorst, the German commander in Strasbourg, ordered the 5,000 men of the 17th SS Panzergrenadier Division into Moussey to flush out the SAS.

Isselhorst's next action was to be swift and brutal. In reprisal for the attack, every male resident of Moussey between sixteen and sixty was rounded up, arrested and interrogated, before being deported to concentration camps in Germany. Two hundred and ten men were taken from Moussey; only seventy would eventually return, two-thirds of the entire male population of the village murdered.

After the atrocity in Moussey, the SAS were no longer viewed with such friendly eyes by the people of Vosges. Prior to Franks' arrival the locals had coexisted with the Germans in a kind of uneasy 'live and let live' arrangement: the farmers, artisans and smallholders of the remote, rural community were not seen as any kind of threat by the occupying army. Now, the war had come to their sleepy villages with a vengeance, and many blamed the British for it.

There were also deeper, more historical factors at play. The story of Alsace is one of centuries of flux between France and Germany. For hundreds of years, as empires rose and fell across Europe, this stretch of the border would move back and forth between the countries; between 1871 and the end of the First World War in 1918, Strasbourg was not even French at all, but part of Germany. Many of the older residents of Vosges still considered themselves German.

This complicated socio-historical make-up of the area was not something Allied Command had considered. And it was to prove fatal.

By the end of September, Franks was in a bind. Not only had it become clear that the US Third Army wasn't coming any time soon, but after the arrest and deportation of the men of Moussey the support of the local Maquis had all but dried up completely. Worse still, despite the sacrifice of the men of Moussey (or perhaps because of it), he suspected that some residents of the other villages were actively working with the Germans to betray his force.

The enemy was closing in on the SAS and the commandos no longer felt safe in the forests they once ruled. Eleven men had already been lost in the operation; now outnumbered, outgunned and constantly looking over their shoulders for traitors, there seemed to be no option for the remaining force but to abort the mission completely.

The only problem was how. Franks' men were still at least

40 miles (64 km) from Nancy, with a whole Panzergrenadier division standing between them and the safety of the American lines.

Reasoning that multiple small groups stood a better chance than one big party, Franks split the commandos into five separate units, each ordered to make their own way to Nancy. Of the eighty SAS troopers who attempted the journey, thirty-four would not make it. And the fate of thirty-one of them would not even be known until after the war.

Three of the commandos had been ambushed and killed almost immediately after setting off from the forest, stumbling into the path of an SS patrol that had been lying in wait for them. Of the other thirty-one missing men, there was no sign.

It took a post-war investigation by Lieutenant Colonel Franks himself to discover what had happened. Heading up the SAS War Crimes Investigations Team, he was told in the autumn of 1945 that the bodies of some SAS men had been found in shallow graves near the German town of Gaggenau, just over the border. After the subsequent arrest of Erich Isselhorst, the truth finally came out.

Isselhorst was the former head of the Gestapo in Munich; in the summer of 1944 he had been posted to Strasbourg, where he took charge of the 'Sicherheitspolizei', or Security Police, a branch of the Gestapo with a reputation for terror tactics. It was Isselhorst who ordered the purging of Moussey – and the subsequent deaths of 140 innocent civilians – and it was Isselhorst who also decided the fate of nearly half of Franks' force.

The SAS's attempted escape west to Nancy was always going to be a battle against the odds. By October the Vosges countryside was crawling with thousands of German troops stationed there against the American advance but all too happy to pursue the British commandos while they waited. Within days, as well as the three killed by the SS patrol, another thirty-one SAS men had been captured and transported to prison in Gaggenau, supposedly for questioning.

Isselhorst had no intention of questioning his captives. On 25 November, the troopers were taken into the forest in groups of three, and shot in the head. For devoted SS officer Isselhorst the *Kommandobefehl* was clear, and he used it to ruthless effect.

The thirty-one murdered men were added to the fatalities already attributed to Operation Loyton. The final tally for the mission read 45 SAS men and 140 French civilians killed. Only 14 of them had died in combat. Most tragically, their sacrifice had achieved little, either militarily or strategically.

Moussey today remains a tiny rural community, little more than a collection of houses and small farms nestled among the Vosges mountains. At a crossroads in the centre of the village there stands a discreet, impeccably maintained memorial to 'Moussey A Ses Martyrs' – the martyrs of Moussey. As well as naming every one of the 140 villagers taken away to be killed in the concentration camps, it includes the names of all the SAS men who died in Operation Loyton, including the thirty-one captured and murdered in cold blood.

OPERATION GALIA

NORTHERN ITALY,
DECEMBER 1944 – FEBRUARY 1945

THE STORMS THAT hit the northern range of Italy's Apennine mountains during the last days of 1944 were especially vicious, even for an area used to harsh winters. For weeks, driving snow and bitter winds sent temperatures plummeting; day and night the skies remained heavy, leaden, never lightening beyond a murky grey. Huge drifts and landslides blocked the high passes, rivers burst their banks, thick snow blanketed the countryside; travelling any distance was like wading through treacle.

It was into these atrocious conditions that thirty-three men from 2nd SAS parachuted into the mountains between the towns of Genoa and La Spezia; and it was under these conditions that they spent seven weeks living rough, running and gunning and frustrating an entire division of 6,000 German troops sent to flush them out.

Northern Italy at the end of 1944 was proving to be a thorn in the side of the Allied liberation of Europe. While American and British forces had pushed the German army from most of France and back to the banks of the Rhine by late autumn, the Italian campaign – begun nearly a full year before D-Day, with the invasion of Sicily in July 1943 – had come to a grim stalemate as the enemy dug in across a defensive line stretching the breadth of the country north of Florence, from Pisa on the west coast to Rimini on the east.

By December 1944 it had been fully fourteen months since the SAS men of Operations Candytuft and Saxifrage had tormented the Germans between Ancona and Pescara, but in that time the Allied armies had pushed little more than 170 miles (274 km) northwards. Now, with Hitler's Italian forces massed behind what was known as the 'Gothic Line', progress had stalled altogether.

The situation was frustrating – but Allied Command feared worse.

On 16 December, the Germans had pushed through Allied lines between Belgium and Luxembourg in the north in what became known as the Battle of the Bulge. Over 400,000 men and 5,000 tanks, artillery pieces and other heavy equipment, surprised the Allies with a devastating counter-offensive through the thick forests of the Ardennes and into Belgium. The attack was finally halted by Christmas, but the speed, ferocity, organization and sheer numbers involved was a rude awakening for Allied Command. The German army was not yet defeated, nor Europe won.

Under no circumstances could a similar counter-offensive be allowed to take place in northern Italy. The answer? Operation Galia – part classic SAS smash-and-burn mission, and part deception campaign. A small team of commandos would be parachuted behind the Gothic Line to disrupt communication and transport links, mine roads and ambush convoys, but they would be doing it as noisily and ostentatiously as possible, so as to fool the enemy into thinking the operation was part of a much larger force breaking through the German lines, and in the process effectively nipping in the bud any plans for an Ardennes-like counter-attack.

It was another mission in which the odds were heavily stacked against the SAS, and it was another mission in which they would defy those odds superbly.

◆ ◆ ◆

On 27 December 1944, as bitterly cold winds howled into the Apennines south of Genoa driving a wall of freezing sleet and snow before them, a lone DC47 'Dakota' twin-engine RAF transport plane scudded across the sky. Battling poor visibility and dangerously unpredictable gusts, the pilot wrestled to keep the aircraft as level as possible – and get his cargo as near to the drop zone as he could manage.

It was touch-and-go stuff, almost the definition of flying by the seat of your pants. One other Dakota had already been blown into the side of a mountain on an earlier reconnaissance flight, and as the heavy aircraft lurched and staggered, lifting and falling with the wind, the men on board – including the pilot – put their trust in luck as much as aviation skill.

Finally, a momentary lull in the gale and the moment was seized: the signal came, and one by one, thirty-three men from A Troop, No. 3 Squadron, 2nd SAS, parachuted from the plane towards what they hoped would be the Rossano valley, 20 miles (32 km) inland from the coastal town of La Spezia, and around 50 miles (80 km) behind the Gothic Line in north-west Italy. As if the conditions weren't dangerous enough, the drop was made in daylight – or what passed for daylight in such conditions.

Despite the heavy clouds and driving snow, each of the

troopers formed clear black silhouettes against the grey sky as they fell, obvious targets for anyone who might be watching. As with Operation Titanic in France six months before, this was to be no undercover penetration into enemy territory: they wanted to be seen.

Miraculously, given what they had jumped into, the team not only landed safely, but did so in the right place: the pilot may have had luck on his side, but he also clearly had an abundance of skill.

Led by Captain Bob Walker-Brown, who had himself escaped from an Italian POW camp in October 1943 and later fought with Major Roy Farran in the Forêt de Châtillon as part of Operations Wallace and Hardy, the men immediately retrieved the supply canisters that had dropped with them (and also somehow landed intact and on target) and made for the rendezvous point, and a meeting with the Italian partisans who were to be their guides through the mountains.

As with the Maquis groups in occupied France, the partisan resistance fighters were an invaluable asset to behind-the-lines commando operations in Italy; tragically, like their French counterparts, they would also pay a heavy price for their cooperation.

The partisans provided maps, local men to act as guides, and locations of safe houses and possible camps, and Captain Walker-Brown laid out his plan. His thirty-three troopers were to split up into six groups: a command section of seven men and then five smaller units, four of five men and one of six. They were to carry out raids and ambushes, sometimes together, sometimes separately, spreading out from La Spezia in the south to Genoa in the north, and inland eastwards towards Parma.

By dividing his men and attacking in different ways, from different locations and at different times, Walker-Brown hoped to give the impression of a much larger force operating in the area – and fool the enemy into thinking that the SAS commandos were in fact a fully intact parachute brigade.

On the morning of 28 December, three sections set off north and east into the mountains; the others turned their attention to the coast, and the strategically vital road from Genoa to La Spezia.

Walker-Brown waited a full day before carrying out his first attack of the operation, in part because he wanted to see if the parachute drop had been picked up by the enemy, and if so, just how big a force they might send to deal with it; and in part to properly reconnoitre the area. The partisans' information seemed to be sound enough, but experience had taught him that there was no substitute for first-hand intelligence.

As it turned out, despite dropping into the Rossano in daylight, perhaps thanks to the terrible weather conditions the troopers' presence in northern Italy did not yet appear to have been noticed: there were no signs of increased enemy activity, and no extra patrols sent into the area to hunt for them. On the night of 30 December, Walker-Brown set about changing that.

As the afternoon gloom gave way to evening proper and the temperature sank below zero once again, the remaining seventeen men who had stayed in the area made their way towards the coast, struggling through snowdrifts and frozen mud, dragging two heavy Vickers machine guns with them to a spot just south of the town of Borghetto di Vara, the main German headquarters for the region.

Walker-Brown had chosen this spot for his ambush carefully. On the one hand, it was tactically sound: not only was the road from Genoa to La Spezia overlooked there by a natural rocky outcrop behind which his team could hide, but it also afforded a good view both up and down the road, meaning little chance of the SAS men being ambushed themselves in reply.

On the other hand, its proximity to Borghetto di Vara was deliberate too. Walker-Brown wanted the Germans to know about the attack, and to fear the fact that it had come so close to their base.

Entrenched behind cover, and with their guns covering the road in both directions, the commandos waited in the cold and relentless sleet, rubbing freezing hands and blowing on numbed fingers, eyes peeled for headlights.

They did not have to wait long. Before an hour had passed, a convoy was spotted, four vehicles from La Spezia, heading for Borghetto. Walker-Brown waited until the lead car was right underneath them before giving the order. Suddenly the mountain erupted, the Vickers sending a volley of lead into the convoy, backed up by the troopers' own machine guns. Their aim was deadly accurate: one vehicle after another caught fire, three exploding outright, and the fourth veering off the road where it continued to burn. Four German soldiers had also been shot dead as they jumped from the vehicles, the rest were running blind towards Borghetto.

Walker-Brown let them run. They could spread the word that the Allies had come, and by the time they had sent a patrol to investigate, he and his men would be long gone, back into the mountains to prepare for their next strike.

◆ ◆ ◆

Operation Galia's first attack had been a success, but things had not worked out so well for another of the SAS teams. The group of six men that had headed east the day before had barely made any progress before being surprised by a faction of Italian fascist soldiers. Surrounded before they could mount any kind of defence, they had no option but to surrender.

The Italians handed them over to a German unit at the town of Montebello di Mezzo, but not before executing their partisan guide. Thankfully, the SAS troopers would escape the same fate, and were instead transported to Germany to see out the rest of the war as prisoners. Had Hitler's deadly *Kommandobefehl* not made it as far as Italy? Or was it because the enemy really did believe the British men to be part of a larger parachute brigade, rather than special forces commandos?

Walker-Brown decided to make up the Germans' minds for them. On New Year's Day he went after Borghetto di Vara itself.

As well as the two Vickers guns, a mortar cannon had been dropped with the troopers, capable of firing heavy shells from 1,000 yards (914 m) with reasonable accuracy. Ideal, in other words, for launching a barrage against an enemy that both outnumbers and outguns you, without having to risk engaging them in direct combat.

Using the atrocious conditions to their advantage, the team were able to make their way down the mountains hidden by the snowdrifts to a spot on the forest's edge close enough to Borghetto – and high enough above the town – for the mortar to be in range. As the first day of the new year turned to night, the revelries of the Germans there were cut abruptly and rudely short by a sudden blitz of destruction.

Thirty shells slammed into the area around the barracks in just a few minutes, smashing into the buildings from seemingly nowhere, sending bricks and masonry and glass flying in a deadly hail of shrapnel.

As the men in Borghetto dived for cover and their officers desperately tried to rally them into some sort of order, the attack stopped, as suddenly and unexpectedly as it had begun. For minutes nobody moved, and by the time they had organized themselves for a counter-attack, the commandos had once again vanished into the forests.

Captain Walker-Brown had made his presence known to the enemy in spectacular style: now he set about making them think his remaining twenty-seven commandos were actually a force of several hundred paratroopers clearing the way for a full Allied assault.

Over the following month his five teams hit a series of targets across the area in a series of devastating raids: while one group stayed to harass convoys on the Genoa–La Spezia road – in one attack killing at least one high-ranking Nazi officer after ambushing his staff car as it raced towards Genoa – others moved inland, mining bridges, attacking railway tunnels and ambushing columns of artillery headed from Parma towards the front.

Hit from all angles, the enemy fell for it: surely no small special forces team could carry out so many attacks simultaneously, and especially in such terrible conditions? German intelligence had reported no push from the Allied front line ... could this be an invasion of north-west Italy from the air?

Just in case they hadn't fully got the message, on 12 January Walker-Brown attacked Borghetto di Vara again, this time killing another fifty-six German soldiers stationed in the town.

The deception worked. Word reached the SAS team that a full division of 6,000 troops had been diverted from the front and into the mountains to flush out what they believed to be a brigade of 400 crack Allied paratroopers.

For the rest of January the German division, bogged down by heavy equipment and sheer numbers, struggled to make headway through the thick snows and forests of the Apennines, as the nimbler, quicker SAS teams, aided by partisan fighters who had lived their whole lives in the mountains, kept one step ahead of them, and even found time to continue their attacks on road convoys and patrols.

Eventually, frustrated at chasing ghosts, the Nazis once again vented their anger on the locals, rounding up and executing suspected partisans, or sometimes just murdering innocent civilians. In his report, Captain Walker-Brown later described discovering the aftermath of one such reprisal by the Germans, noting: 'In one village we went through I saw the bodies of around twenty young men and girls who had been machine gunned to death against a cemetery wall.'

Far from crushing their spirit, such displays of wanton brutality only strengthened the partisans' resolve, and made the SAS men even more determined to inflict as much damage on the Nazis as possible.

Finally, on 10 February, after seven weeks of raiding and running in Arctic conditions on the mountains, surviving on iron rations and with the constant danger of enemy attack, Captain

Walker-Brown received the order to withdraw. Operation Galia had done everything and more expected of it – and his men, by now half-starving, frostbitten and exhausted – had performed above and beyond the call of duty.

Of the thirty-three SAS commandos who had dropped into the storms above the Rossano valley on 27 December, only the six captured troopers failed to make it back to Allied lines. Between them they had inflicted more than 150 casualties on the enemy, as well as destroying over twenty vehicles and blowing up numerous strategically important roads, railway lines and bridges.

More importantly, they had successfully fooled the German army into thinking they were a full-blown force of more than 400 men – and for much of January had tied up an entire 6,000-man division in the mountains that would otherwise have been fighting on the front.

Captain Bob Walker-Brown was immediately awarded a Distinguished Service Order for his leadership of the mission, with the citation paying tribute to his 'unparalleled guerrilla skill and personal courage' in keeping his men alive and fighting for over two months in abominable conditions.

OPERATION COLD COMFORT / ZOMBIE

NORTHERN ITALY, FEBRUARY–MARCH 1945

CAPTAIN WALKER-BROWN and his twenty-seven men had barely made it back to Allied lines before another SAS party was despatched to the far north of Italy. Operation Galia had successfully put paid to any ideas of a German counter-offensive in the country; now the Allies were preparing for a decisive assault on the Gothic Line themselves.

What would become known as the Allied Spring Offensive (official title: Operation Grapeshot) was scheduled for April 1945, and Command wanted not only to finally push the Germans from Italy once and for all, but also to ensure that as few Nazi divisions as possible made it back across the Alps to Germany itself.

One of the keys to achieving both those aims was the destruction of the Brenner Pass, the only major transport link between Italy and Austria, and the main route for German armies either reinforcing the front, or else retreating back to the Fatherland. Block or blow up the Brenner Pass, and the Germans would effectively be isolated in north Italy, caught between the mountains and the advancing Allied armies.

For Major Roy Farran, veteran of Operations Candytuft and Saxifrage, hero of Wallace and Hardy, and now in charge of all SAS operations in Italy, it seemed a no-brainer that the task of taking out the Brenner Pass should fall to the SAS.

Under the operational name Cold Comfort, a party of twelve men led by Captain Ross Robertson Littlejohn would parachute into the countryside east of Lake Garda, and with the assistance of the local partisan fighters, make their way 40 miles (64 km) north through the mountains to a spot near the town of Bolzano. It was here, as the main road and rail routes to the Brenner Pass followed the Adige river valley, that the commandos would strike.

Dominating the skyline near Bolzano was a huge rock pinnacle towering over the valley below: if Littlejohn's team could blow that pinnacle and trigger a landslide, then thousands of tons of rock would be sent crashing into the valley, choking the road, destroying the railway line and damming the river. The Brenner Pass would be unusable for months.

After the triumphs of Operation Galia, Major Farran was confident that Cold Comfort could repeat its success – and in Captain Littlejohn it had the kind of daring and resourceful leader on which the whole ethos of the SAS itself had been based.

Littlejohn was still just twenty-three years old, but he already had a fearsome reputation. He had won a Military Cross for his actions on D-Day, when, as part of 4 Commando, he had stormed Sword Beach in the initial wave of landings. Despite his unit suffering 50 per cent casualties in the assault, Littlejohn had broken through enemy lines to take out an entire German bunker single-handedly, and escaped capture by playing dead – even as enemy soldiers stuck him with their bayonets – before crawling a mile (1.6 km) through the fighting back to Allied lines.

After his recovery he joined the SAS, where it was decided that Cold Comfort was to be exactly the kind of do-or-die mission that suited his unique talents.

As with previous operations, the Cold Comfort force was to land in two waves. A party of four including Littlejohn would parachute into the mountains on 17 February, where they would contact the local partisans and establish a base, followed by the greater force of eight men a week later.

Unfortunately, things started badly ... and deteriorated from that point on.

◆ ◆ ◆

The freezing storms that had plagued Captain Walker-Brown's men the month before had spread to cover all northern Italy – and without a pilot as skilled, or as lucky, as Operation Galia's, both parachute drops missed their targets by miles. Worse, in the high winds and driving snow, their accompanying supply canisters were blown wildly away or else smashed on the mountains, meaning the men were left without suitable clothing for the sub-zero conditions, the necessary explosives to carry out their mission, or even properly functioning radios to contact HQ for further supply drops to replace them.

The weather was not the only challenge Littlejohn's team faced. Once again British intelligence had failed to properly understand the social demographics of an occupied area so close to the German border. This far north, the local people were far less keen on helping the Allies than they had been in the Apennines: not only were the partisan fighters that had proved so vital to previous operations altogether rarer in this part of the Italian Alps, but many actually identified more with the Germans and Austrians, with whom they had been coexisting for centuries, than with the 'invading' British and Americans.

As Littlejohn's team (dropped too far east) and the rest of the force (dropped too far west) attempted to make their way towards a rendezvous near the town of Trento, the partisans, when not openly hostile, were not exactly helpful. The SAS were essentially on their own.

For days, Littlejohn's four-man unit struggled through the snow without any supplies or winter clothes other than had been on their person when they landed. Only two of them made it to Trento. Splitting up to reconnoitre the best path through the treacherous frozen mountainside, Littlejohn and another man, Corporal Joseph Crowley, were surprised by a ski unit of Italian fascists. Typically for Littlejohn, they put up an almighty fight, killing and injuring several of the Italians, but the situation was hopeless: outnumbered and out of ammunition, they had no option but to surrender. The Italians took them to Bolzano, where they were handed over to the SS.

The remainder of the force had little better luck. Also badly in need of proper clothing, food and other kit, they established the best kind of base they could manage in the forests south of Trento and hunkered down in the hope that Littlejohn might yet join them.

He never did. On 19 March, he and Corporal Crowley became the latest victims of Hitler's *Kommandobefehl*, executed in cold blood by the SS.

For the remaining troopers, Cold Comfort was essentially over – so much so that it even acquired a new operational name even more darkly appropriate than its original: Operation Zombie.

Leaderless, lacking explosives, ammunition and equipment for the freezing conditions, starving, frostbitten and exhausted, the men slowly made their way south again.

Ten of the twelve commandos who had parachuted into northern Italy to blow up the Brenner Pass survived the mission, but none ever came within 50 miles (80 km) of their target, and in the capture and subsequent murder of Major Littlejohn, the SAS needlessly lost a natural-born leader who might have gone on to become a key figure in the force's future success.

Major Farran vowed not to allow the same mistake to happen again. Next time, he was going to take personal charge of the operation – on the ground, where it mattered most.

OPERATION TOMBOLA

ITALY, MARCH–APRIL 1945

AT 02.00 HOURS on 27 March 1945, the 300 German soldiers garrisoned in the sleepy town of Albinea, 50 miles (80 km) north-west of Bologna, were woken by a noise none of them had ever heard before. Cutting through the chilly night air came a deep, throaty drone, and then above it, a soaring, stirring wail ... surreally, spookily, the sound of the Scottish Highlands, come to the hills of northern Italy.

A lone bagpiper stood, dressed in full uniform of the Highland Light Infantry – complete with kilt – at the entrance to the town, belting out the 'Highland Laddie' for all he was worth.

And then all hell broke loose.

Albinea was a German stronghold for the region between Bologna and Parma, and as well as being home to 300 elite Mountain Corps soldiers, also served as headquarters for several high-ranking officers. The troops were billeted in several buildings in the south of the town; the officers and their staff commandeered a pair of grander buildings in the centre, the Villa Rossi and the Villa Calvi.

The sentries guarding those buildings died before the piper blew his first note. As they fell, attack teams made up of ten SAS commandos and twenty Italian partisan fighters stormed each of the villas, grenades ripping rooms apart, guns blazing wildly.

Although they had been sleeping just seconds earlier, the forty men inside quickly organized themselves; the SAS took the ground floors with ease, but a fierce firefight erupted on the staircases, bullets ricocheting off the walls, grenades tossed both upstairs and downstairs, smashing and splintering and blowing apart the grand marble walls and antique furniture. Bodies on both sides fell.

From the lawns outside the villas, another thirty SAS troopers unleashed a torrent of heavy machine-gun fire, as well as rockets from a bazooka, into the upper floors of the buildings. Masonry and bricks and plaster flew.

The sudden explosion of noise and light and bagpipes also woke the men in the barracks to the south: 300 battle-hardened Mountain Corps soldiers grabbed their weapons and raced towards the clamour ... only to be met by a roadblock. Behind it, a troop of Russian escaped POWs with vengeance on their minds and British guns in their hands. The first wave of Germans fell like dominoes, the rest dived for cover under a hail of bullets, unable to get near the officers' buildings.

After twenty minutes of fierce fighting, Major Roy Farran gave the signal. As the commandos still fighting in the villas piled furniture and files and whatever else might burn and then soaked them in petrol, a single flare was fired into the sky above Albinea; the fuel was ignited, the buildings burst into flames, the bagpiper finally fell silent, and the attackers withdrew.

As they melted back into the dark, the wreckage of the Villas Rossi and Calvi burned bright and loud behind them. The screams of the men trapped inside were audible even above the continuing blasts and explosions.

◆ ◆ ◆

If the SAS had learned one thing from the debacle of Operation Zombie, it was the importance of winning over those Italians in the north whose instinctive sympathies were with the Germans. Without help from the partisans, deep-penetration missions in the mountains were near-impossible; but at the same time, with the Nazis increasingly savage in their reprisals on anyone suspected of helping Allied commandos, local support was in danger of drying up completely.

To counteract this, Major Farran – whose exploits in the Forêt de Châtillon had secured his promotion but also gained him a reputation as a maverick – came up with a novel means of convincing the enemy that any attacks behind their lines were definitely the work of the British army ... and only the British army.

His solution: a bagpiper. Farran not only wanted the Germans to know they were being attacked by the British; he wanted those attacks to be soundtracked by the most British noise imaginable. No German alive was going to be mistaking a brawny Scot in a kilt belting out the 'Highland Laddie' for an Italian partisan.

For what was to be the SAS's final operation in Italy before the Allied Spring Offensive, Farran was determined to put the disaster of Operation Zombie behind him and get back to what the elite unit was best at: a series of 'who dares wins' lightning strikes designed to instil as much terror and confusion in the enemy as cause material damage.

On 4 March, fifty SAS men would be dropped into the countryside near Reggio Emilia, close to the area where

Captain Bob Walker-Brown had performed such heroics during Operation Galia a few months before. After establishing a base in the mountains, they would attempt to win over and organize the partisan fighters and with them inflict as much damage on the Germans ahead of the Spring Offensive as possible – thus not only ensuring that enemy troops were diverted away from the front line to deal with them, but also sowing chaos and uncertainty in the German retreat itself.

As it turned out, the operation was to be more swashbuckling than even Major Farran could have imagined. The men of Tombola were to be perhaps the strangest fighting unit of the war – and certainly the oddest in SAS history. They were also to be one of the most spectacularly successful.

After landing, Farran's men successfully pulled together a force of over a hundred Italian partisans together with seventy escaped Russian POWs. All were eager to fight: the Russians, who had endured the horrors of the Nazi invasion of their country and then terrible conditions in the prison camps, were especially fierce. They were led by a man called Victor Pirogov, a blond giant who rechristened himself 'Victor Modena' after the Italian town.

Farran duly gave his ragtag army a unique name too: the 'Battaglione Alleata', or Allied Battalion, and requested further air drops of weaponry and supplies to equip them with, as well as David Kirkpatrick, of the Highland Light Infantry, and his bagpipes.

If the Battaglione Alleata were a disparate force, they looked it too: while Kirkpatrick had his kilt and the SAS troopers their battledress and berets, the Italians and Russians wore whatever they had looted, a mix of Russian, American and German uniforms all at once, embellished with bandanas, bushy beards and a bewildering array of hats. Victor Modena finished his look off with a bright sash of blue parachute silk wound around his neck.

In the Forêt de Châtillon Major Farran had played at being Robin Hood. Now he had a real-life band of outlaws under his command. Not least among them, Farran himself. His very presence in the hills of Reggio Emilia put him at risk of court martial. His attack on Albinea, doubly so.

◆ ◆ ◆

From the very beginnings of Tombola's planning, Farran had wanted to take personal command of the operation on the ground, but his request was flatly rejected by Allied Command, who – perhaps in part due to the loss of Major Littlejohn just weeks before – felt that he was too important an officer to be risked. By way of compromise, they did allow him into the aeroplane to accompany the men on the drop, but with the strict warning that on no account was he to parachute himself.

What happened next depends on who you believe ... and how far your credulity is prepared to stretch.

In his official explanation, Farran later claimed that during the flight and just as the aircraft approached the drop zone he had tripped and accidentally fallen out of the plane along with his men, and it was just sheer good luck that he happened not only to be wearing a parachute at the time, but also to have his full battle-ready kit to hand, too.

Once he was on the ground, of course, there was little sense in trying to extract him, but he was told in no uncertain terms that he was treading on thin ice, and would have to account for his actions should he survive the operation.

Effectively disobeying a direct order and passing it off as an accident might work once, but as befits the leader of a band of Merry Men, it would not be Farran's only act of insubordination during Operation Tombola.

The attack on Albinea was to be the first major test of Farran's Battaglione Alleata, but this too had also been expressly vetoed by Allied Command. Although initially given the green light, intelligence learned that the Germans were planning a sweep of local villages for partisan rebels and, fearing reprisals, ordered Farran to call off the attack until 9 April and the start of the Spring Offensive.

The major ignored the order – and would later claim that by the time he learned of it, it was too late anyway – despite knowing that a court martial would be a distinct possibility if he should ever make it back to Allied lines.

Not that he cared about any of that at the time. In the immediate aftermath of the attack, back in their hidden base in the mountains, Farran was too busy celebrating with his guerrilla army to worry about the stuffed shirts back behind the lines. As the wine flowed and Kirkpatrick piped a succession of ever-more uproarious reels; as Italians, Russians and British men drank and laughed and even danced together; the most frequent toast was two shouted words, in Italian: 'Battaglia Alleata! Battaglia Alleata!'

Albinea had been an outrageous success: as many as sixty Germans had been killed or badly wounded, the regional chief of staff Oberst Lemelson was dead, and the whole enemy headquarters burned to the ground, along with countless maps, operational orders and other documents. In reply, the SAS lost just three dead and two wounded, and the partisans only five wounded. In addition, the ruse with David Kirkpatrick had worked: far from being a commando raiding party backed up by a motley crew of Italian partisans and bloodthirsty Russians, the Germans believed the attack to be evidence of a full Scottish paratrooper regiment in the region, perhaps even the vanguard of the main Allied army itself. No partisan or special forces raiders would dare assault such a large German garrison so openly ... and certainly not with a bagpiper in attendance.

No reprisals were inflicted on the civilian population as a result. And the partisans – not to mention Victor Modena's seventy Russian fighters – were firmly and devotedly Major Farran's men.

◆ ◆ ◆

For the following month, Farran's picaresque army cut a swathe through the Germans in the Apennines west of Bologna. The Spring Offensive finally launched on 9 April, and as the Germans were beaten back from the front line, the Battaglia Alleata spread fear and havoc among the retreating troops. Further air drops had boosted their firepower and provided them with jeeps, and so confident was Farran in his men that he repeatedly engaged the enemy from open positions, on one occasion killing fifty German soldiers without a single Allied loss.

On 20 April, with US troops now through the Gothic Line defences and making rapid headway through northern Italy, Farran upped the ante still further. Attacking the German base at Albinea had been bold, but launching an all-out assault against the much larger city of Reggio Emilia – even with his private army now numbering close to 250 partisans, Russians and SAS troopers – was borderline madness.

On 20 April, the Battaglia Alleata set up their heavy weapons – a 75-mm (3-inch) pack howitzer and a 10-lb (4.5-kg) mortar cannon – in the hills above Reggio Emilia. Farran gave the signal and they unleashed a barrage of shells into the main city-centre square and prepared for a fight. For two hours, Farran's men shelled the city; when they finally stopped – slightly mystified at the lack of response from the enemy – they discovered that the German garrison had fled after the first mortars fell, believing the attack to be a full-blown US armoured division rolling into town.

Somehow, the Battaglia Alleata had liberated Reggio Emilia without even engaging the enemy. Some thought it hilarious; others, Victor Modena included, were disappointed at the lack of a good scrap.

Farran's band of outlaws were to have one last triumph before finally being overtaken by the Allied armies. On 22 April word reached the partisans that a huge column of German trucks, tanks and other vehicles was retreating along Highway 12, the main route north to Verona, Lake Garda and the Austrian Alps beyond. The sheer number of vehicles – plus the presence of dozens of horse-drawn carts – meant the convoy was all but crawling along, and therefore ripe for ambush.

It was too good a target for Farran to pass up. Immediately mobilizing his forces, he raced towards Modena, and a spot near the bridge at the town of Sassuolo. As they hid in the hills, the retreating column could be seen stretching for miles, inching their way towards the bridge.

With Farran commanding one section and Victor Modena taking the other, the Battaglia waited for the order to strike. Farran delayed the signal until the bridge was fully loaded, and then, at 14.30 hours, in the balmy broad sunshine of a beautiful Italian spring afternoon, unleashed hell.

The mortars pounded, the howitzer howled, and every man with a machine gun unloaded all they had into the convoy. The effect was instantaneous, and, for the Germans at least, horrific. Trucks and cars exploded, horses stampeded, tanks ground uselessly to a halt, dozens of enemy soldiers died where they fell. Farran did not let up until he had exhausted his ammunition.

◆ ◆ ◆

Operation Tombola was finally wound up on 24 April, after a month in which Major Farran's swashbuckling, piratical Battaglia Alleata had become a terror for the last of the German fighters in northern Italy. For the loss of just twenty-four men across the SAS, partisan and Russian divisions of his force, they had killed an estimated 300 enemy soldiers, destroyed dozens of trucks and other vehicles, demolished at least one major regional HQ and taken hundreds more Nazis prisoner.

Just as importantly, their presence around Reggio Emilia had been a nightmare for the enemy, a phantom army bringing death and destruction accompanied by the eerie, haunting skirl of bagpipes. As Farran pointed out in his report, the fear and confusion they created in the retreating troops undoubtedly hastened the US army's advance through northern Italy.

Back behind Allied lines, however, there was still music to be faced. Tombola may have been an outstanding success, and

Farran's command of his ragtag brigade an astonishing example of leadership, but there was also the small matter of his having disobeyed a direct order not to attack Albinea, to say nothing of the fact he was not even supposed to have been there in the first place.

Major Farran ended Operation Tombola believing he would face court martial. As it turned out, that was to be another impossible situation he somehow emerged from unscathed. He was let off with a verbal dressing-down, his excuses conveniently believed. A rogue he may have been, but he was a brilliant SAS operative too. Once again, the two seemed to go hand in hand.

Eight days later, on 2 May 1945, Field Marshal Harold Alexander, commander of the Allied armies in Italy, sent out a 'Special Order' to every Allied soldier in the country. Surviving original copies are still held in museums and by collectors today. 'After nearly two years of hard and continuous fighting ... you stand today as victors of the Italian campaign,' it read. 'You have won a victory which has ended in the complete and utter rout of the German armed forces in the Mediterranean.'

The war in Italy was over – thanks in no small part to the often-hidden heroics of the SAS. But Germany was not yet defeated. And the SAS would still have one more memorable part to play.

OPERATION ARCHWAY

GERMANY, 25 MARCH – 8 MAY 1945

AT ALMOST EXACTLY the same time as Major Farran's Battaglia Alleata was swashbuckling through the Apennines, another SAS operation was underway 700 miles (1,126 km) north, in Germany itself.

On 22 March, US forces had crossed the Rhine at Nierstein, near Frankfurt; the following night the main Allied army under the command of Field Marshal Bernard Montgomery did the same 200 miles (322 km) downstream, at three points near the Dutch border. The invasion of Germany, and the final phase of the war, had begun.

Montgomery had assembled a huge number of troops for his attack on the Fatherland – a million men in what was to be the largest amphibious assault river crossing in history – but he also knew that the river guarding Germany's border was only the first hurdle on the long road to Berlin. The writing may have been on the wall for Hitler, but not everyone in the Third Reich was prepared to concede the war was lost. At the very least, they were not going down without a fight.

The field marshal highly valued the SAS from his battles with Rommel in the desert, and for his final push he devised the most wide-ranging and ambitious SAS endeavour of the war. Operation Archway was to be a far cry from the fast, mobile, run-and-gun raids the unit had become famed and feared for – instead, two full squadrons numbering some 300 commandos mounted in seventy-five jeeps armed with Vickers machine guns and 3-inch mortars would provide reconnaissance and support for the Allied advance all the way from the banks of the Rhine to the heart of Berlin. As it turned out, they would also fulfil a very different, unexpected, and more lastingly significant role along the way.

◆ ◆ ◆

Operation Archway was executed two days after Montgomery's assault on the Rhine. The SAS commandos crossed the river on 25 March and split into two parties; arrowing ahead of the advancing main force, their role was to reconnoitre enemy positions and strength, and – old habits dying hard – inflict what damage they could on the retreating or entrenched Nazis along the way.

For twenty-one days the SAS squadrons cut through Germany, clearing a path for Montgomery's army, until, on 15 April, with Nazi resistance dwindling, one such reconnaissance mission chanced upon a find that would change the course of history.

In those three weeks the Allies had advanced 200 miles (322 km) – roughly half the distance to Berlin – and Archway's roving jeep patrols had increased in frequency, range and ambition: with the enemy on the run it was now not unusual for parties as small as two men to scout out an area unaccompanied.

It was under these circumstances that Lieutenant John Randall and his driver zoomed through the woods near the town of Bergen when they noticed a large iron gate guarding a seemingly innocuous track into the trees.

Why would such a nondescript track need such an imposing gate? Randall decided to investigate.

At the end of the road was what first appeared to be a prison camp. But as he later described to Alexander van Straubenzee of the *Daily Telegraph* in a 10 April 2005 interview, Randall quickly realized that they had chanced upon something else entirely.

'We were totally unprepared for what we had stumbled across,' he said. 'About thirty yards [27 m] into the camp, my jeep was suddenly surrounded by a group of around 100 emaciated prisoners. Most of them were in black and white prison uniforms and the rest wore a terrible assortment of ragged clothes. It was the state of these inmates that made me realise that this was no ordinary POW camp.'

As he continued to investigate, worse horrors were to be revealed. Some of what he described remains difficult to read even eight decades later.

'About thirty yards on we came across an even more pathetic sight,' he remembered. 'Groups of almost naked skeletal figures, pulling clothes off dead bodies and trying to clothe themselves ... Dead bodies, mainly naked, were strewn around ... The stench was horrific. It was a mixture of rotting flesh and excrement.'

Aghast, Randall radioed back to base, and thirty minutes later was joined by squadron leader Major John Tonkin, the veteran commander who had barely escaped the murder of his thirty-three men during Operation Bulbasket.

As the four SAS men stood speechless before the hellish scene, they were approached by a German officer who introduced himself as Josef Kramer, the camp commandant, and a woman named Irma Grese, who said she was responsible for the female prisoners. Extraordinarily, the smiling Kramer offered the British commandos a tour of the camp.

Tonkin not only declined the invitation, he promptly arrested both Kramer and Grese, and claimed the prison camp, which we now know as Bergen-Belsen, under the protection of the British army.

By the time Field Marshal Montgomery arrived at Bergen-Belsen a few hours later, some 60,000 prisoners had been discovered at the camp. Another 60,000 are now known to have died there, piled into mass graves or simply left to rot where they fell. Among them was the diarist Anne Frank, who had perished just weeks before Randall's patrol happened to drive by.

Montgomery never forgave the Nazis for what he saw at Bergen-Belsen. Under his direct order, court proceedings were immediately initiated against officers at the camp: eleven of them, including Josef Kramer and Irma Grese, were hanged for their crimes.

'During the years of the Nazi regime in Germany, things happened which could not find a parallel in the most debased days of the Roman or Mongol empires,' Montgomery later wrote. 'Crimes were committed which most people could not imagine, unless they had seen a place like Belsen, which I entered on the day of its liberation by my troops in April 1945. The wholesale liquidation of civilians was unprecedented.'

Belsen was the first of the Nazi concentration camps to be liberated by the British, and was a significant step in the discovery of the full horrors of the Nazi holocaust.

◆ ◆ ◆

On 30 April, with the Third Reich in tatters and all of Germany under the control of the Allies to the west and the Russians to the east, Adolf Hitler committed suicide. Eight days later, his successor, Grand Admiral Karl Dönitz, surrendered unconditionally. Three months after that, in the wake of the atomic bombings of Hiroshima and Nagasaki, Japan followed suit. Twelve years of terror and atrocity that had begun with Hitler's rise to power in 1933 and culminated in the bloodiest war in human history, had finally come to an end. Some 75 million men, women and children had been killed during the conflict, of which 50 million were civilians.

With the German surrender came a reassessment of the role of the SAS. The special forces unit dreamed up by David Stirling, and which had produced such mavericks as Paddy Mayne and Roy Farran, had played an invaluable role in the Allied victory. From its inception with Operation Squatter in November 1941 to the end of Operation Archway three and a half years later, the SAS had suffered 330 casualties – but in response had killed or wounded nearly 8,000 enemy soldiers, and captured a further 23,000.

The force had performed far above and beyond the wildest expectations of Allied Command, but now, with the Nazis defeated and peace in Europe, it seemed there was to be no further need for such a specialized unit. On 8 October 1945, all regiments were disbanded.

As it turned out, it was not to be the end for the SAS. It was just the end of the beginning.

PART 2

GLOBAL THREATS

OPERATIONS HELSBY ET AL.

MALAYA, FEBRUARY 1952 – FEBRUARY 1958

THE SAS HAD first been formed with a very specific purpose in mind, and if the unit had subsequently evolved to meet the changing challenges of the Second World War, its essential ethos remained the same: mobile, high-risk missions undertaken by highly trained individuals prepared to put everything on the line to achieve their goals.

If the Ministry of Defence thought the need for such a specialized force had ended with the conclusion of that war, however, they were wrong.

In the years following 1945, a new threat to national security emerged. In the chaos of Germany's retreat, Russian premier Joseph Stalin had taken the opportunity to greatly expand the Soviet Union – the immediate concern for the British and Americans now was not fascism, but communism.

The war had also exposed the frailties of the fading British Empire, spread out across the world and viewed increasingly as anachronistic and even dictatorial. In 1948 those two elements blew up together in the territory of British Malaya.

Chin Peng, Leader of the Malayan Communist Party, formed a rebel militia calling itself the Malayan National Liberation Army, set up a network of hidden bases in the jungle and launched a war of independence against the British.

The troops stationed in the country could not cope with the insurgents' guerrilla tactics and superior knowledge of the terrain; and with the situation worsening, General Sir John Harding, Commander-in-Chief Far East, asked Major Mike Calvert, a veteran of jungle warfare in Burma, to come up with a plan.

Calvert's conclusion: what was needed was a dedicated force that could not only operate for extended periods in the jungle, but work with local tribespeople to help track down, flush out and counter-attack the communist rebels.

In 1950, the SAS was back in action, under the name the Malayan Scouts (SAS).

◆ ◆ ◆

Calvert got to work immediately on his two-pronged approach. Establishing a headquarters near the town of Ipoh, around 120 miles (193 km) north of Kuala Lumpur, he sent regular fourteen-man patrols into the jungle: they were charged not only with tracking those rebel groups that intelligence already knew about, but also to try to win the trust and support of the local tribesmen.

It was a painstaking process, but the sensitive approach gradually began to pay dividends, with the establishment of medical clinics in the jungle villages – often the first time many there had any kind of access to basic dentistry or trained midwives – proving especially effective.

It was a two-way relationship. As the SAS provided medical care, so the aboriginal tribes taught the commandos jungle survival and tracking techniques passed down through countless generations. Before then, the accepted wisdom was that no British unit could last more than seven days safely in the Malayan wild:

under the instruction of the tribesmen, Calvert's men learned to survive for weeks, even months, off-grid.

In tandem with this 'hearts-and-minds' campaign – similar to the wartime relationships built up with the French Maquis and the Italian partisan fighters – the SAS put their new skills to the test in a series of more 'traditional' missions, the first of which was given the codename Operation Helsby.

In early 1952, raids by the Malayan National Liberation Army in the remote Belum Valley, near the border of Thailand, had become increasingly ambitious in range and size, even threatening to overrun the area completely. In response, the SAS were to parachute in, use the new skills and knowledge they had acquired from their jungle training to track down the insurgents, and, backed up by a separate ground force of Royal Marines and Malay police, destroy their base and kill or capture as many of the rebels as they could.

The operation was not a great success: of the sixty SAS troopers parachuted in to the jungle, only four landed safely. The rest became tangled in the thick jungle canopy – by the time they had managed to descend, any element of surprise was lost and the terrorists mostly fled. Sure enough, the valley was secured and the rebels' base destroyed, but few of the enemy had even been seen, let alone engaged.

On the other hand, valuable lessons had been learned. The debacle of the parachute jump brought about two changes that would revolutionize SAS operations for the future.

First, every man who jumped into the jungle from that point on did so equipped with a length of rope up to 49 metres (160 feet) long, meaning he would be able to quickly abseil down from the trees if he got snared.

The second came in 1953, with the arrival of military helicopters. Suddenly the commandos could penetrate deeper into the jungle without the need to parachute at all. 'Fast-roping' – literally sliding hand-over-hand down a rope hanging directly from the chopper itself – was a dangerous, but incredibly effective method of landing large amounts of troopers far quicker and more accurately than any parachute drop could ever hope to.

Through the following years, the British ground down the communist uprising, gradually regaining control of the country. The SAS had played a key role militarily, with regular sweeps of the jungle pinning down the insurgents or else forcing them to stay constantly on the move, but it had also been instrumental in the political battle for Malaya. The hearts-and-minds campaign had proved hugely effective – the medical clinics they brought to the protected villages attracted more and more local people to them, effectively removing great swathes of the populace from the danger of becoming drawn into or caught up in Chin Peng's revolution, and denying the rebels the shelter and supplies they might have otherwise got from them.

By 1958 the insurgency was over, and the SAS campaign wound down. Their final tally was fewer than 100 terrorists killed, but the real value of the unit's operations in Malaya were less quantifiable – and more significant – than numbers of enemy killed or material destroyed. By learning valuable new skills, techniques and means of operating in the field, most especially jungle survival and warfare, the SAS had not only secured its future, but laid the groundwork for some of the most daring missions the force was to undertake in the decades to come.

OPERATION CLARET

INDONESIA–MALAYSIA BORDER, 1964–66

FEBRUARY 1965, and in the jungles of north-east Borneo, four men from 'D' Squadron SAS crouched on the edge of a bamboo patch, listening.

The jungle is never quiet. A dizzying barrage fills the air twenty-four hours a day – the calls and cries of orangutans, macaques, proboscis monkeys and gibbons, the endless shrieks of the millions of hornbills high in the rainforest canopy.

Hundreds of feet below the clamour, the troopers remained motionless. Despite the noise they nevertheless strained their senses, tuning out the din, watching and listening for anything unusual.

Led by Sergeant Edward Lillico, they were on a patrol across the Malaysian border into Indonesia, following the Sekayan River near Gunong Rawan, or 'Melancholy Mountain', looking for evidence of enemy activity in the area. Their presence in this part of the jungle was not only top secret, but the subject of plausible deniability at the highest level: officially, the SAS were not in Indonesia, had never been in Indonesia, and were certainly not engaged in any kind of armed conflict with soldiers from the Indonesian army. It would take until 1974 before any Claret operations were publicly disclosed by the British government.

Lillico watched as lead scout Iain Thomson looked back and

nodded – the signal that he was going to make his way through the bamboo towards the abandoned camp the patrol had sighted the night before. Behind him the other two troopers prepared to follow.

Thomson did not even have time to raise his rifle before a new sound ripped through the air: sharp, staccato barks of automatic fire. Struck in the thigh, he hit the floor, blood already seeping through his uniform. Lillico dived to his right but caught another bullet in his left hip. As he fell he saw his lead scout snatch up his weapon and unload into an Indonesian soldier, who had stood, thinking he had felled both men.

The sergeant followed suit, ignoring the searing pain from his side and shooting towards the camp and whatever enemy hid there, inching backwards on his stomach towards the trees and some kind of cover.

Somehow, both he and Thomson made it to a dense patch of jungle, and settled into a makeshift foxhole to defend the position. Both were badly injured and took turns to provide covering fire while the other dressed their wounds as best they could. Neither were able to stand, and only a tourniquet had saved Thomson from a catastrophic loss of blood. Behind them, the other two troopers had not got involved and instead fell back to the emergency rendezvous point: if it seems now like running from a fight, it was not – standard procedure dictated that retreating for backup and reinforcements was vital in ambush situations.

The two men were alone, in hostile territory on the wrong side of a border they had officially not crossed, under attack from an unknown number of enemy soldiers, and bleeding heavily. The prognosis was not good.

◆ ◆ ◆

By the early 1960s Malaya had become Malaysia, following a negotiated treaty that saw the country gain independence, while remaining part of the Commonwealth and a continuing strategic base for British forces in south-east Asia. But with that new status came other tensions – most notably with neighbouring Indonesia, whose president Ahmed Sukarno resented the continuing British presence in the region. In 1963, even as the Vietnam War to the north was escalating into a major conflict, he launched 'Konfrantasi', a clandestine and undeclared war along the Malaysia–Indonesia border across Borneo, between the communist-sympathizing Indonesian army and the Commonwealth forces on the island.

Officially, there was no armed conflict, but simply an escalation of troop activity on both sides. On the ground, it was a different story. British intelligence deemed the Indonesian army to be on the brink of a major territorial land grab, the consequences of which would not only be disastrous for the emergent Malaysian federation, but threaten the stability of all south-east Asia.

Somehow the Indonesian army had to be stopped, but without the situation blowing up into a full-scale conflict that could drag the whole region into an extended Vietnam-style war.

The SAS's jungle experience learned in Operation Helsby made the force the natural choice for such a covert operation: in July 1964, Major General Walter Walker, Director of Borneo Operations, ordered a campaign of undercover, top-secret patrols and raids under the codename Operation Claret.

The SAS was charged with pinning down the Indonesian army

along the length of the border, but to do so without attracting too much attention, or giving President Sukarno an excuse to launch an all-out war in Borneo.

Claret remains one of the strangest episodes in the history of the SAS – in no small part because the level of secrecy was so high that nobody outside those directly involved even knew it had happened at all until a decade later.

The secrecy was further maintained by the strict limits imposed on the men on the ground. Rather than engage the Indonesian forces in open combat, SAS and other Commonwealth troops would instead operate in small units from a series of bases along the border, penetrating the jungle to hit enemy camps and patrols just hard enough to keep them busy, but not so aggressively as to antagonize Sukarno into escalating the conflict.

These cross-border raids were limited to a range of 5,000 yards (4,572 m), or just short of 3 miles (4.8 km), and every man was instructed that on no account were casualties, including the dead, allowed to be taken by the enemy. There were literally to be no prisoners.

The first raids from Operation Claret began in the summer of 1964, and would continue for two years. In February 1965, it was to be the turn of Sergeant Lillico's squad.

◆ ◆ ◆

Lillico's orders had not been to engage the enemy directly, but rather to monitor their movements and reconnoitre the area around the Sekayan River, where intelligence had reported a build-up of Indonesian troops. If their presence was discovered they should defend themselves, but also withdraw back across the border immediately. As an emergency last resort, Lillico, as commander, had been issued with a search-and-rescue beacon: turning it on would transmit a signal with his location so a rescue party could be sent out.

The party of eight men had made steady and unremarkable progress through the jungle towards the river, but after nearing the limit of their 3-mile (4.8-km) incursion zone, chanced upon what looked like an abandoned enemy camp. A cluster of empty bamboo huts stood lopsided and collapsing around a clearing; inside one the team could make out rusted tins of food and other litter.

Watching from the safety of the jungle, there seemed no evidence of any recent activity, but Lillico wasn't taking any chances. With the light fading, he ordered his men to retreat to their own secured camp. The following morning he, Thomson and two other men would return to investigate further – the other four troopers would stay behind just in case anything went wrong. At the first sight or sound of trouble, they were to return to the rendezvous point.

Whether the 'abandoned' enemy camp was a deliberately sprung trap, or whether it just so happened that an Indonesian patrol saw Lillico coming and improvised an ambush, will forever remain unknown, but as the two men lay in the jungle, badly wounded and pinned down under heavy fire, Lillico reflected that, either way, the bottom line was the same. They needed to get out of there, and they needed to do it fast.

Thomson's tourniquet was holding up well; with a bit of luck and a lot of effort, he reckoned he could make it back to the rendezvous point. Lillico, on the other hand, could barely move: his hip wound was still bleeding, despite the field dressing. Together, the two men made a plan.

As Lillico unleashed a torrent of bullets towards the camp, Thomson crawled back the way they had come, towards the border. It was tortuous going; unable to put any weight on his injured leg, he was forced to move on his elbows, every yard an agony, trusting in blind faith to avoid any snakes, scorpions, spiders or other venomous nasties lurking in the undergrowth.

The covering fire continued until he was out of sight, and then the sergeant looked to his own safety. Still letting out sporadic bursts from his machine gun, he edged back into the jungle, searching for a place to lie up and hide.

He and Thomson had taken out at least three men, but with his ammunition almost spent, he knew he could not hold his position much longer. It was only a matter of time before the rest of the enemy patrol made a close sweep of the area to mop up any survivors, and his orders were clear. On no account were SAS men to be discovered in Indonesian territory – alive or dead. He would hide as best he could, try to survive the night, and if he was still alive in the morning, activate the emergency beacon and hope to God his men could get him out.

Finally, some good fortune. Just a short way into the forest was a huge fallen tree trunk; using his hands as shovels, Lillico spent the last of his energy burrowing out a hole underneath it, before smearing camouflaging mud on his hands and face and sliding into it, dragging what branches and leaves he could to hide himself.

What followed was the longest night of Sergeant Lillico's life. Lying still for hours in a muddy hole underneath a tree trunk would be uncomfortable at the best of times; doing so in the Borneo jungle at night, with the threat of snakes and scorpions – not to mention bigger predators such as clouded leopards, bay cats and sun bears – was almost unbearable; suffering all of that while bleeding from a bullet in your hip and knowing a party of enemy soldiers are hunting for you with the revenge of three of their fallen colleagues on their minds, was more than any man should have to endure.

And yet, somehow, Lillico did endure. And as the misty light of a February dawn filtered through the jungle canopy, there finally came the sound he'd been praying for: the unmistakable rhythmic whirl of a Westland helicopter. Right then, the most beautiful noise he'd ever heard.

All he had to do was switch on the emergency beacon and the chopper would pick up the signal, drop a rescue crew, winch him up, and he would be home and dry.

Unless ...

What if the Indonesian patrol was still close by? It had only been one night, after all, and it was most likely that after sweeping for him they had camped in the area. There was every chance they were still near enough to hear the chopper too, and if they did, would relish the chance to spring another ambush.

In those circumstances, activating the beacon would not only fail to save Lillico, but actually endanger the lives of more British soldiers. Swearing silently, lengthily and bitterly, the sergeant left the transmitter switched off, closed his eyes and as the sound of the helicopter gradually faded away, once again tried to blank out the pain.

By the time he heard it return, Lillico could no longer tell if the light was fading because it was evening, or because the loss of blood meant he was losing consciousness. The answer was both. A full night and day had passed since his party had been ambushed; surely the enemy patrol would have moved on by now?

One last effort, that's all that was needed. One more thing to do. One final, Herculean labour.

Sergeant Lillico reached into his pocket, flicked the switch, activated the beacon, and, trying not to scream in agony, dragged himself out of his hole far enough for the rescue team to find him. Minutes later, he heard a British voice, and finally passed out.

◆ ◆ ◆

Lillico woke in a hospital bed back at the British base in Kuching, 70 safe miles (112 km) from the border. Next to him was Iain Thomson. Against all the odds, both men had somehow survived. For their bravery, Thomson received a Mention in Despatches and Lillico was awarded the Military Medal.

The following October, President Sukarno was overthrown in a military coup, and on 28 May 1966 Operation Claret was suspended. A week later, Indonesian radio announced peace between Indonesia and Malaysia.

It would take another decade before tensions in south-east Asia eased enough for the SAS's presence in Borneo to even be acknowledged, and for the heroics of men like Thomson and Lillico to be revealed. Even today, just how many missions were undertaken in those two years remains unclear – as well as how many other extraordinary stories remain lost to the jungle.

THE BATTLE OF MIRBAT

OMAN, 19 JULY 1972

BY 1972, the SAS was more than thirty years old, but, despite David Stirling and Paddy Mayne's unconventional band of brothers establishing itself as the most formidable and capable special forces in the world, few people outside the military even knew it existed at all.

The subterfuge that had been so important when fighting Nazi Germany had extended into post-war operations – though now the secrecy was due more to political than military necessity. Operations Helsby and Claret had shown that the force had a vital role to play around the world, and had also illustrated the importance of often having to do so without anyone ever hearing about it.

On 19 July 1972, those two apparently contradictory principles were to collide in what for many historians remains the SAS's finest moment.

The regiment had been sent to the mouth of the Persian Gulf in strictest secrecy. The Sultan of Oman was fighting against communist insurgents from the Popular Front for the Liberation of the Occupied Arabian Gulf, who were also known as the 'Adoo', meaning simply 'enemy' in Arabic. Officially, the British were not involved on the ground, but helping only in an advisory capacity; in reality, the SAS were there to train the pro-Western Sultan's forces – and, if needed, get stuck in where it mattered most.

The Oman capital Muscat was of huge strategic and economic importance for the West: if it were to be taken by the communists, the supply of oil from the Persian Gulf through the Straits of Hormuz would be cut off. Holding the city was vital.

By July 1972 the situation had become perilous. The rebels had gained control of much of the desert, and with it the confidence to attack more open and heavily defended positions. And they were steadily making their way to Muscat.

Standing between the insurgents and the capital was the sleepy fishing village of Mirbat, and a small garrison of nine SAS troopers.

The British men were based in a building just outside the town known as the BATT (for British Army Training Team) House. Their defences were minimal: a barbed-wire perimeter fence, a single heavy machine-gun nest, a lightweight 81-mm (3-inch) infantry mortar, and, 500 metres (547 yards) from the house, a gun pit containing a 25-pounder (11.5-kg) anti-tank artillery cannon – a heavy, near-obsolete relic from the Second World War designed to fire across distances up to seven miles (11 km). Each man also had a rifle and grenades, and their leader, Captain Mike Kealy, a twenty-three-year-old on his first detachment to the SAS, carried an additional pistol.

Nearby was a post from the Omani Army known as the 'Night Picket'. They were supposed to be the first defence against any attack. As it turned out, they were to be the first casualties of the Battle of Mirbat.

◆ ◆ ◆

In the cold hours before dawn on 19 July, a raiding party of Adoo assassins crept up to the Night Picket and ruthlessly, silently, slit the throats of the guards, before slaughtering the remaining men. The main force followed behind them: 250 rebel fighters armed with Soviet-made AK-47 assault rifles and backed up by mortar cannons.

As the nine SAS men slept in the BATT House, the guerrilla army massed along the perimeter fence, setting up their mortars, waiting for the signal to attack.

At a little before 06.00 hours, they opened fire. The ground around the house erupted as a barrage of mortar bombs tore into the flimsy defences; simultaneously, wave after wave of Adoo fighters charged on the British base.

Captain Kealy's men were caught unawares – but not for long. Within seconds of the first shell landing, they were up and racing for position, Kealy barking orders and each man obeying without question or hesitation. By any standards, the situation was hopeless – what could nine men do against 250? – but none of these SAS troopers were about to flinch from their duty. They were here to defend Mirbat, and they would do so to the very last man, whatever the odds.

Corporal Bob Bennett and trooper Roger Cole dived into the machine-gun nest, one manning the Browning, the other greasing the ammunition. The two British-Fijian commandos with the squadron, Trooper Sekonia 'Tak' Takavesi and Sergeant Talaiasi 'Laba' Labalaba, along with one other trooper, raced for the mortar pit. Kealey and the remaining men took up position behind sandbags on the roof, switching off the safety catches of their self-loading battle rifles and aiming at the advancing Adoo.

They didn't waste time. As Tak and Laba launched a returning volley of shells from the mortar – aiming by sight to save precious seconds – Bennett and Cole's Browning machine gun spat out deadly bursts at the enemy, raking down the rebels as they tore and clambered through the barbed-wire fence. From the roof, the other men took more careful aim, trying to pick off targets one by one.

The SAS were putting up a hell of a fight, but for every man they felled a dozen others came behind. Even with the Browning now on constant fire, it was only a matter of time before they were overwhelmed by sheer numbers.

Kealy got on the radio to HQ, shouting to make himself heard above the rattle and roar of bullets and bombs. Despite the din, he spoke with the kind of lucidity that only comes from years of training, calmly explaining the situation and requesting backup, by airstrike preferably, and as soon as possible.

Meanwhile, in the mortar pit, Laba, a giant of a man and a veteran of the Borneo campaigns, decided on a more immediate course of action. Leaving his Fijian countryman and the other trooper to man the mortar, he made a dash for the 25-pound artillery gun: if he could bring that weapon into play, it might swing the odds at least a little more in their favour.

Reaching it meant a 500-metre (547-yard) run across open ground. With a grin and a slap on Tak's back, he slung his rifle over his shoulder and sprinted through the bullets.

Somehow, he made it, sliding into the pit under a hail of fire and immediately set about loading a shell. The huge weapon was designed to be crewed by at least four men and preferably six – showing superhuman strength, Laba somehow managed to load and fire it all by himself, pointing the barrel almost horizontally, smashing out a round a minute across the sand, sending bodies flying.

Corporal Peter Warne, who was on the roof with his rifle, later described the scene to the *Fiji Times* in an article dated 26 October 2018.

'As the adrenaline kicked in the emotional shutters came down and all feelings of humanity were locked out,' he remembered. 'It's a kind of exhilarating insanity, it's kill or be killed. So we set about taking them out. The group in front were hit, the line faltered then wave upon wave of them were advancing, grabbing at the barbed perimeter wire with bare hands while Laba was blasting them into oblivion.'

In Laba's hands the artillery weapon had become an instrument of awe and terror, its shells, designed for penetrating thick armour across huge distances, instead slamming into waves of human bodies, one destructive minute after another.

Manning the gun single-handedly was an extraordinary achievement; getting off a round a minute was near-miraculous, but it was still not enough. The Adoo, realizing that stopping the weapon was the key to winning the assault on the BATT House, shifted their attack: they now threw everything they had at the artillery pit.

Still, Laba held them off. Until, all at once, the big gun fell silent.

From a third of a mile (half a kilometre) away the troopers back at the house couldn't make out the situation around the 25-pounder. Sekonia Takavesi didn't wait to find out. In a flash he was out of the mortar position and racing across the ground to his countryman; caught by surprise by the dash, the attackers didn't notice him at first – by the time they turned their bullets on Tak he'd made it, diving head first behind the sandbags.

He found Laba alive, but horrifically injured. A bullet had ripped through his jaw, tearing half his lower face to shreds. He was dazed, in agony, but clasping his friend, he stood up and once again, loaded a shell into the gun.

The two Fijians got back behind the artillery piece and rejoined the battle, the waves of Adoo so close now they were firing blind, no longer needing to aim, loading and blasting the anti-tank cannon point-blank.

'When Laba and I were firing we were under heavy attack,' Takavesi later told the *Fiji Times*. 'They were almost on top of us, shooting from all directions. We were firing at point-blank range, we had no time to aim ... We were pretty short of ammunition and the battle was getting fiercer. They were still advancing, and we were almost surrounded. Then Laba told me there was a 66-mm [2.6-inch] mortar inside the gate.'

Behind the artillery gun, across open ground, was another pit, containing more ammunition and another mortar. Laba, despite his injury, set off to get it, crawling on his hands and knees as shells and bullets rained down around him.

'We were joking in Fijian and I said, "Laba, keep your head down" as he crawled away towards the mortar,' remembered Tak. 'I was covering him then I heard a crack, I turned, all I could see was blood. A bullet had hit Laba's neck and blood was spouting out.'

From the BATT House roof, Captain Kealy saw the big sergeant downed. The gun fell silent again, and only the intermittent crack of Tak's rifle from the emplacement showed that he was still alive. Once again, someone had to make that third-of-a-mile dash to the artillery pit and get the weapon going again ... and this time the enemy would be expecting it.

Kealy did not hesitate. With the mortar now manned by a single trooper, and Bennett and Cole still firing the Browning, he asked for a volunteer from the remaining three men to accompany him on what would almost certainly be a suicide run.

Every man put his hand up.

Kealy selected Tommy Tobin, a trooper with medical training, and together they ran, dived, crouched and crawled their way through the storm, leaping over shell blasts, ducking under bullets, returning fire when they could. A good athlete in perfect conditions can make the distance in around ninety seconds; Kealy and Tobin were good athletes, but they had been fighting a desperate battle for hours now, and these were not exactly ideal conditions.

A ninety-second sprint was never an option. It took a little longer, but, despite the chaos, against all the odds, both men made it.

As they slid into the pit, they were greeted with a grin and a grimace by Tak. The Fijian had taken a bullet through the shoulder and another had grazed the back of his head; unable to work the big gun, barely able to stand, he had propped himself up against the sandbags and was using the last of the ammunition from his rifle, firing in tight, controlled bursts at the attackers.

Kealy joined him, cutting down men as they appeared at the very lip of the emplacement, while Tobin crawled over to check on the fallen Laba. It took just a moment to establish the big

Fijian was dead, and as Tobin crawled back another bullet hit him in the face. He fell into the pit, alive but mortally wounded.

The situation was now desperate. Kealy and Takavesi were almost overwhelmed, and even with the SAS mortar now targeting the area directly in front of the artillery gun – a dangerous, high-risk move, as one misjudged shell would see their own men blown up – the Adoo continued to pour through the breached defences. Within minutes it would surely all be over.

And then ... a miracle.

Roaring low out of the clouds, two Strikemaster attack jets from the Omani air force, cannons blazing. Kealy's call for help had finally been heard. For thirty minutes the jets ran pass after pass, strafing the rebel army, scattering bodies before them.

The Strikemasters were not the only reinforcements. Appearing over the hill behind the insurgents came a column of soldiers from 'G' Squadron SAS.

It was too much for the Adoo. With the planes spitting fire on them from above, and caught between the renewed fury of Kealy's men in front and the relief squadron of fresh SAS commandos behind, they turned tail and fled.

◆ ◆ ◆

For seven furious hours, Captain Kealy's nine heroes had held back 250 bloodthirsty rebels. They lost just two men in the battle – Sergeant Labalaba and Trooper Tobin, who later died of the bullet he had taken while trying to reach Laba. Official records show the bodies of thirty-eight Adoo fighters were recovered, though many on-the-ground estimates put enemy casualties at twice or three times that number.

The Popular Front for the Liberation of the Occupied Arabian Gulf never recovered from the defeat: after the Battle of Mirbat, the sultan's forces slowly regained the ground they had lost to the insurgents, eventually driving them from Oman altogether.

For Kealy and his men, credit for their extraordinary efforts was, at least at first, kept muted. It would not be until three years later that the British acknowledged that the SAS had even played a part in the Omani war at all, and the story of the Battle of Mirbat could finally be told.

Even today, controversy remains over the lack of proper recognition for the defenders of Mirbat. Although Captain Kealy was awarded the Distinguished Service Order, Troopers Sekonia Takavesi and Tommy Tobin a Distinguished Conduct Medal each (in Tobin's case posthumously) and two of the other men a Military Cross each, for his part in single-handedly manning a Second World War anti-tank gun against the horde of communist rebels, Sergeant Labalaba received only a posthumous Mention in Despatches.

In 2018, the Duke and Duchess of Sussex unveiled a memorial to Talaiasi Labalaba in Fiji, at a ceremony where fellow guests included Fijian President Jioji Konrote, and Laba's old friend Takavesi. There remains a campaign for Laba to be awarded the Victoria Cross, the highest and most prestigious award any member of the British armed forces can receive.

LUFTHANSA FLIGHT 181

MOGADISHU, 18 OCTOBER 1977

THE SAS HAD for decades been Britain's most potent secret force, operating undercover and often unofficially around the world to protect the security of the West, but as the century progressed, the nature of their duties naturally diversified. They couldn't get involved in every emergency, but, especially in the case of Britain's strongest allies in the Cold War, they could work with foreign special forces units to pass on a little of their expertise.

On a runway in Mogadishu in October 1977, in tandem with the nascent West German special force *Grenzschutzgruppe 9* (or GSG-9), the SAS demonstrated how these 'instruct and observe' partnerships could work against an insidious new threat: terrorism targeted against innocent civilians.

GSG-9 had been formed in the aftermath of the attack by Palestinian terrorist group Black September during the Munich Olympic Games in 1972. Eight members of the organization had stormed the Olympic Village, killed two members of the Israeli Olympic team, and taken another nine athletes and coaches hostage.

The West German police force's attempt to rescue the hostages was a disaster. Woefully undertrained, unprepared and under-equipped for such an operation, they tried to ambush the terrorists; in the resulting firefight, all nine hostages were massacred, five terrorists were killed, and one German police officer fatally shot.

The tragedy led the West German government to create a dedicated unit, specializing in combating hostage-taking, kidnapping, extortion and terrorism. As part of the post-war conditions imposed on the country, the new unit could not be part of the army – and so the *Grenzschutzgruppe*, translated as 'Border Protection Group', officially formed as a wing of the police force. Unlike the SAS, they were prohibited from engaging in military conflicts, but that didn't mean they couldn't work with, and learn from, the British elite force. And, when it came to an emergency, they weren't too proud to ask the SAS for help.

Their first test was to come just five years after the Munich attack.

◆ ◆ ◆

At 11.30 hours on Thursday 13 October 1977, a Palestinian calling himself 'Captain Martyr Mahmud' calmly walked up the aisle of a Boeing 737 passenger plane as it passed over Marseille, en route from Palma de Mallorca to Frankfurt, Germany. On board with him were eighty-six passengers, mostly German holidaymakers returning home, as well as five crew.

At the door to the cockpit he paused for a second. Behind him, three other Lebanese members of the militant group Popular Front for the Liberation of Palestine unbuckled their seat belts, stood, and spread out along the plane.

All at once, Mahmud – real name Zohair Youssif Akache – burst into the cockpit brandishing a loaded pistol, dragged the co-pilot Jürgen Vietor out of his seat and shoved him back into the economy section of the plane. At the same time, his three colleagues moved up and down the aisle with their own weapons drawn, knocking over drinks and food trays, screaming at the passengers to remain in their seats with their hands up.

Akache pointed the pistol at pilot Jürgen Schumann and ordered him to change course. Lufthansa flight 181 was no longer going to Germany – they were now headed for Larnaca, Cyprus, with a stop at Rome to refuel.

It was at Rome that the hijackers made their demands. They wanted US$15 million (roughly $74 million today), as well as the unconditional release of twelve political prisoners: two Palestinians held in Turkey and ten members of the Red Army Faction, a radical far-left German terrorist group also known as the Baader-Meinhof Group. Should these conditions be met, and only if they were met, the hostages would be released.

It was also at Rome that the West German authorities made their first play. Interior Minister Werner Maihofer did not want to negotiate with terrorists. He asked the Italians to shoot out the tyres of the plane to prevent it taking off.

The Italians refused. This was not a fight they wanted to be a part of – least of all in the Eternal City. Flight 181 could be somebody else's problem. Fully refuelled, the 737 took off again that evening, heading for Larnaca.

What followed was an increasingly tense series of stop-offs as the terrorists headed haphazardly eastwards. From Larnaca, Akache tried to land in Beirut, Damascus, Baghdad and Kuwait – only to be refused permission by air traffic control for each of the airports, some even blocking the runways with tanks and military jeeps. The plane did manage to touch down for fuel in

Bahrain, Dubai and Aden before finally landing in Mogadishu, capital of Somalia, at daybreak on 17 October.

Minutes after touching down, Akache activated the right rear emergency evacuation slide. As the Somali troops surrounding the plane watched, the lifeless body of pilot Jürgen Schumann was thrown down. He had been shot in the head at point-blank range. Akache and his companions were now not only hijackers, they were murderers.

By this time the terrified passengers and crew had been confined to the aeroplane for four full days with minimal food, water or toilet access. They had also witnessed the cold-blooded execution of their pilot, and heard the terrorists' repeated threats that unless their demands were met, more murders would follow.

In Mogadishu, Akache issued his final demand. Unless the Red Army Faction prisoners were released by 02.30 the following morning, he would blow up the plane, killing everyone inside. In order to ensure there would be no survivors, all the duty-free spirits on board were smashed open, and the hijackers poured the flammable liquid over their hostages.

But as the terrorists had made their chaotic way across Europe and the Middle East to Somalia, the West Germans had not been idle.

Colonel Ulrich Wegener, overall commander of GSG-9, had assembled a team of thirty commandos to follow Akache's movements since the hijacked plane had left Italy. To support his task force he also requested two men from the SAS.

Wegener's original plan was to have his commandos storm the aircraft in Dubai while they attempted to refuel. The Dubai government agreed, but the SAS troopers did not. They had been invited by Wegener to join the team in an advisory role, 'observers' rather than combatants, and it was a responsibility they took as seriously as if Lufthansa flight 181 were a British plane and any rescue attempt a wholly SAS operation.

The GSG-9 unit was not ready, they argued. More combat exercises and dry runs on an identical dummy 737 were needed before any live attempt could be made to free the hostages. The hijackers had to be hit hard, hit fast, and hit decisively. A disaster like that of Munich five years before had to be avoided at all costs.

For forty-five hours out of the following eighty, under intense supervision from the SAS, the GSG-9 commandos were put through their paces. Four decades of high-risk undercover operations around the world had made the SAS experts in springing traps and executing ambushes, of launching surprise assaults and overwhelming enemies before they had time to react. Now they had no more than a few days to pass on as much of that experience and know-how as they could to a team that only had one shot at getting it right.

Again and again the GSG-9 operatives were run through the best means of storming the aircraft, again and again they familiarized themselves with the minutiae of the plane's interior layout, again and again they rehearsed how to adapt to every possible scenario that might meet them once the order was given to attack.

At 20.00 hours on 17 October, a little over twelve hours after Akache's hijackers landed at Mogadishu airport, another plane touched down on the tarmac, easing on to the runway with all lights off, a ghost ship in the darkness. Inside were thirty GSG-9 commandos and two SAS men. In total silence, they unloaded and prepared to put their plan into action.

Six hours later, they were ready. The 'Go' signal was given and several things happened almost simultaneously.

First, Somali soldiers lit a fire around 60 metres (66 yards) in front of the plane – a diversionary tactic as basic as it was effective: three of the hijackers rushed to the cockpit to see what was happening.

Next, the German officials who had been negotiating the supposed release of the Red Army Faction prisoners in exchange for the hostages contacted Akache on the radio. A plane containing the prisoners had just taken off from Cairo, he was told, it was on its way to Mogadishu and the arranged hostage swap. What they needed from him now was a detailed explanation of how exactly the exchange was going to proceed.

With Akache tied up on the radio and the other three hijackers craning their necks to see forward out of the cockpit window, GSG-9 moved in from the rear.

Silently climbing the fuselage using blacked-out aluminium ladders with rubbered ends coated in KY Jelly to muffle any noise, one team led by Colonel Wegener made for the forward cabin door, while two other groups crept over the wings to the emergency doors on each side of the plane. Dressed all in black with blacked-out faces, they each carried an automatic weapon and had authorization to use deadly force. As their SAS instructors would have told them: there's a time for sentiment, and there's a time for doing whatever's necessary to save innocent lives.

At precisely 02.07 hours, all three doors were opened at the same time and the commandos stormed inside.

The need for stealth had passed. Now they shouted. *'Wir sind hier um euch zu retten! Runter!'* We're here to save you! Get down!'

The passengers did as they were told. The hijackers, panicked and disoriented, did not, and opened fire.

All those hours under the intense instruction of the SAS paid off. The GSG-9 commandos replied with deadly accuracy, staying calm, picking their targets, making sure they did not miss. Two of the terrorists were killed instantly, the other two fell injured – in Akache's case, fatally.

Just five minutes after crashing through the doors, the backup crew on the ground received the codeword they had been waiting for. '*Frühlingszeit! Frühlingszeit!*' Springtime! Springtime!

Moments later, Wegener radioed the West German chancellor himself. 'Four opponents down. Hostages free. Four hostages slightly wounded. One commando slightly wounded.'

The hijacking of Lufthansa flight 181 was over. All eighty-six passengers were escorted from the plane safely: thanks to the guidance and experience of their SAS instructors, GSG-9 had carried out the rescue without a single civilian casualty and only a minor injury to one of their own. Of the four hijackers, only one survived – albeit with severe bullet wounds to the legs and lungs – and was later imprisoned. Akache died of his injuries before the sun rose on 18 October.

The operation was not only the first significant success for West Germany's newly formed special forces unit, it also reinforced the skill and expertise of the SAS in an era where the threats to national security were evolving in new and terrifying ways. The SAS was never exactly a conventional warfare unit, but as both their role in this operation, and their actions in their next test would show, they were now able to operate with devastating effect in just about any situation.

And it would be that next operation that would propel Britain's elite forces unit out of the shadows and into the consciousness of the whole world.

OPERATION NIMROD:
THE IRANIAN EMBASSY SIEGE

LONDON, 30 APRIL – 5 MAY 1980

A BALMY MAY BANK holiday evening in affluent west London, and outside the Iranian embassy, a five-storey Victorian Grade II listed building overlooking Hyde Park, a sea of television cameras, reporters and press photographers were all focused on the same thing. The feed from their cameras was being relayed live to millions across the country and the images were unlike anything television had ever broadcast before. All of Britain was holding its breath.

On the roof of the building, men from 22 SAS were running through their final preparations. Abseil lines were attached and double-checked, weapons secured, ammunition pouches readied, flashbangs, grenades and explosive charges set in place. The soldiers wore black body armour, balaclavas and gas masks and each was armed with an MP5 automatic machine gun, as well as 9-mm Browning pistols. Further teams waited behind and to the side of the building.

Inside were twenty terrified hostages including embassy staff, visitors, students, academics, journalists and a British police officer. For six days they had been imprisoned by gunmen from the Democratic Revolutionary Front for the Liberation of Arabistan, an Iraqi-sponsored terrorist organization. One hostage had already been murdered; the increasingly frantic terrorists were now poised to kill them all.

At 19.23 hours precisely, the order came. 'Go! Go! Go!' and, live on national TV, the SAS launched their attack.

◆ ◆ ◆

The siege had begun at 11.30 hours on 30 April, when six Iranian Arab terrorists burst inside the Iranian embassy at 16 Princes Gate, Kensington, quickly tackling the sole guard, PC Trevor Lock of the Met Police's Diplomatic Protection Group. Led by Oan Ali Mohammed, a former political prisoner and fervent campaigner for the independence of the Iranian province of Khūzestān, they were armed with submachine guns, pistols and grenades, smuggled into the country via an Iraqi diplomatic bag. As they rounded up everyone inside the building into a single room, Oan loosed a volley from his machine gun into the ceiling to show he was serious.

The gunfire did not go unnoticed: within minutes police had surrounded the embassy, alerted also by the panic button on PC Lock's radio. Before he was overpowered, Lock had managed not only to press the alarm, but also to conceal his own revolver. The latter action was to prove hugely significant.

As the authorities closed in, Oan laid out his demands. He wanted the release of ninety-one Arabs held in Iranian prisons, safe passage from the embassy for himself and his fellow terrorists, and, most ambitiously, independence for Khūzestān. He also set a deadline: noon the following day. If his conditions were not met by then, he would blow up the building and kill everyone in it.

The situation had escalated into a full-blown political crisis.

As the British government assembled an emergency COBRA committee, including Brigadier Peter de la Billière, Director of the SAS, the Iranian government announced that not only did it have no intention of releasing any prisoners (and certainly not of giving up the oil-rich territory of Khūzestān), but it also suspected the whole thing to be a joint MI5 and CIA set-up designed to destabilize its regime.

This was to be a British problem – and it was up to the British to deal with it.

The first priority for those on the ground was to ensure the terrorists did not carry out their threat; the second was to determine exactly what the situation inside the embassy was. As de la Billière explained to COBRA: knowing exactly how many hostages and how many terrorists were inside that building – and, ideally, where inside the building they were – was crucial to the success of any rescue attempt.

At that stage, the SAS were, officially at least, only present as part of the COBRA team. A specialized section of the force called the Counter Revolutionary Warfare Wing had been formed in the 1970s to focus on anti-terrorist and hijacking situations, but, for the moment, the hostages in the embassy were still the responsibility of the police. As a military organization, the SAS needed permission from the Met before it could act on home soil, and the Met needed authority from Prime Minister Margaret Thatcher before they could give it.

Nevertheless, the experience and expertise the SAS provided – not least after its role in assisting GSG-9 in Mogadishu three years earlier – meant that it remained highly involved at every level of the COBRA meetings, and behind the scenes, Lieutenant

Colonel Michael Rose, Commander of 22 SAS, was confident that, sooner or later, the force would be called upon to act.

He wanted his men to be ready for that call. Two teams of commandos were ordered to London, where they set up base, first in Regent's Park and then, creeping from the back in the dead of night, into 14 Princes Gate, next door to the embassy.

Back on the ground, the information de la Billière needed was not long in coming. Late in the afternoon on the first day of the siege, Oan had released embassy press officer Frieda Mozaffarian, after she became increasingly unwell. The following day she was joined by BBC journalist Chris Cramer, who had been visiting the embassy to secure a visa to Iran. He had faked an illness in order to pass on intelligence to the police.

Cramer later remembered: 'I was escorted to an ambulance ... I said, "I want to talk to someone now. Stop the ambulance, you know, there are gunmen in there with hand grenades and there are six of them," and I was terrified that they were going to storm the embassy thinking maybe there was only one or two ... "You need to get word to the authorities that there are six extremely well-armed gunmen in there," and he stopped the ambulance and he jumped out.'

The police had also tracked down the embassy caretaker: he told them that any assault by the front door would be fruitless – following recommendations made by, ironically, the SAS themselves, it had been reinforced by a steel security door. In addition, the ground and first-floor windows had been fitted with armoured glass.

As police continued to negotiate with Oan, with further deadlines being set, missed, and set again, the SAS put themselves on immediate readiness. Two teams were formed: one stood on high alert at 14 Princes Gate, ready to storm the building in case the terrorists started shooting, the other, still in Regent's Park Barracks, painstakingly rehearsing a more considered assault. Full-size replicas of each floor were hastily constructed, as well as a scale model of the building as a whole. Additionally, using the information Chris Cramer and Frieda Mozaffarian had provided, the troopers studied photographs of each of the hostages intently, searing their likenesses into memory: if it came to it, in the heat and confusion of a firefight, they needed to know instantly who was friend and who was foe.

Two more days passed; negotiations continued. On 3 May, four days into the siege, the police succeeded in securing the release of two more hostages. By then the area around the embassy had become a twenty-four-hour-a-day swarm of cameras and reporters. The world's media had descended on Princes Gate, and even in an era before rolling news, were covering every development intently.

That evening the SAS made a breakthrough. Creeping across the terrace rooftops, they discovered a skylight in the embassy roof. Although locked from the inside, by painstakingly picking apart the lead waterproofing around the edge of the glass, they were able to remove a pane and reach inside to disable the lock.

Now they had a guaranteed entry point.

The following day another hostage was released, but by the morning of 5 May, Oan had become dangerously unstable. Frustrated at the continued stalling tactics of the negotiators and increasingly paranoid that the building was about to be attacked, at 13.00 hours he issued an ultimatum: unless an Arab ambassador was summoned to speak to him within forty-five minutes, he would execute one of the hostages.

No ambassador came, and at 13.45 exactly, surveillance reported hearing three shots from inside the embassy.

COBRA held another emergency meeting. A tipping point had been reached, a red line had been crossed. It was now down to the British authorities to act, and act decisively.

Lieutenant Colonel Rose got a message out to his men: he wanted them ready to go at ten minutes' notice. As COBRA discussed whether to finally sign over authority to the elite unit, Brigadier de la Billière warned the prime minister that an SAS assault could mean up to 40 per cent of the hostages being killed.

Shortly before 19.00 hours the door to the embassy opened and the body of Abbas Lavasani, the embassy's chief press officer, was dumped out. He had been shot twice in the head and once in the chest.

Prime Minister Margaret Thatcher uttered three words. 'Yes, go in.'

At 19.07 Deputy Assistant Commissioner John Dellow, the ranking police officer on the scene, signed over control of the operation to Lieutenant Colonel Rose. The SAS had their authorization. Operation Nimrod was on.

◆ ◆ ◆

Everything then happened in a blur, action across all levels of the embassy occurring simultaneously and at dizzying, often improvised, speed.

Immediately upon receiving the order, the four-man team on the roof swung into action, throwing their ropes and abseiling down the rear of the building, heading for the second-floor windows. According to the plan, as they entered the building another four-man team was to throw a stun grenade through the skylight, and the team on the ground floor blow out the rear door.

But then a snag. One of the abseiling ropes tangled, leaving a man dangling in mid-air – as his fellow commandos swung over to assist him, a window was accidentally smashed ... the element of surprise was lost, the terrorists would surely know they were under attack. Worse – with a man still swinging above them, the ground-floor team didn't dare use their explosive charges; instead, they levelled a sledgehammer at the door, praying it hadn't also been reinforced with steel.

Their prayers were answered: the door buckled and caved, and as the charges on the second-floor windows exploded, a fourth team at the front of the embassy simultaneously blew out the first-floor windows, clambering over the balcony in full view of the television cameras and jumping into the building.

The SAS were now in the embassy across four floors and moving fast through the rooms on what one trooper later called a 'search and destroy' mission. One of the terrorists had been taken out on the ground floor, five remained.

There were other problems. The explosive charges had set fire to curtains and bookcases on the first and second floors, and with the building ablaze, every second counted. Not only was there the danger of being caught in an inferno, but the terrorists, knowing their number was up, would surely try to kill as many hostages as possible before they died.

Forty per cent casualties was the expected risk. They could not afford to let 40 per cent become a best-case scenario.

Meanwhile, as the SAS began their assault, PC Lock seized his chance. Throwing himself at Oan, he rugby-tackled his kidnapper to the floor, finally pulling out the pistol he had kept hidden for six long days. Lock had the terrorist leader pinned down when a stun grenade suddenly detonated; the flash and bang had their desired effect ... but on the wrong target. Disoriented, Lock let go of his man, and Oan levelled his own gun at the brave police officer.

And then a shout. 'Trevor! Get away!'

Lock made a desperate roll; behind him, in the doorway, a figure all in black, with balaclava, gas mask and MP5. Before Lock could wonder how the SAS man knew his name, a burst from the MP5 smashed into Oan, killing him instantly.

In another room, two of the remaining terrorists had gathered the male hostages together and started shooting – one man died and two others were injured before the SAS reached them.

Just six minutes had passed since the 'Go!' order and the SAS were now in control of all levels of the building. Four of the six terrorists had been neutralized, but two remained unaccounted for.

The immediate concern was getting the hostages out of the embassy, now burning dangerously out of control. The troopers formed a human chain on the stairs, passing the hostages along the line one to another. Suddenly one of them saw something that made his blood run cold. Concealed in the hands of one of the men shuffling down the stairs, the detonator cap of a fragmentation grenade.

He had no idea if the pin had been pulled, and there were too many bodies around to take the shot – so he instead smashed his MP5 on the back of the man's head and kicked him down the stairs as hard as he could. As he hit the bottom another trooper emptied a magazine into him.

The terrorist's hand opened and, as if in slow motion, the grenade rolled out ... and the troopers breathed again. The pin was still in.

The final kidnapper was discovered hiding among the hostages as the SAS troopers checked each of their identities in the garden at the back of the embassy. He was immediately arrested and later sentenced to life imprisonment.

At 19.40 hours, Operation Nimrod was declared over. Five of the six terrorists were dead and the other in custody. One hostage had been killed, and two others injured. Of the twenty men and women still imprisoned inside the Iranian embassy, the SAS had rescued nineteen. Brigadier de la Billière's warning of a possible 40 per cent casualty rate had been reduced to just 5 per cent. From start to finish the operation had taken just seventeen minutes.

The whole raid had been broadcast live by both the BBC and ITV – the only two national networks on British TV at that time – and watched by millions. The SAS, until then the British military's deadliest and best-kept secret, was suddenly headline news.

OPERATION PARAQUET

SOUTH GEORGIA, 21–25 APRIL 1982

THE IRANIAN EMBASSY SIEGE had thrust the SAS into the public eye for the first time – and the regiment was suddenly overwhelmed with applicants desperate to be a part of the balaclava-clad, MP5-toting force. On the one hand, the fame was welcome – if nothing else, it at least secured the continued existence of the unit – but on the other, being in the spotlight was deeply uncomfortable for a force that, by history and definition, had always thrived on secrecy, working in the shadows, relying on stealth and surprise as much as superior training. Amid all the attention, what most SAS troopers really wanted to do was get on with their job.

In 1982 they not only got their wish, but did so in circumstances that harked back to the very roots of the regiment.

For ten weeks that year, the SAS would not be involved in terrorist or hostage situations, nor be observing, training or covertly engaging in foreign governments' hostilities, but instead fighting in a war for Britain once more.

◆ ◆ ◆

On 2 April 1982, an invasion force of Argentinian commandos bolstered by the 2nd Marine Infantry Battalion landed on the Falkland Islands, a British-dependent territory 300 miles

(483 km) east of Argentina in the South Atlantic.

The tiny islands had a population of just 3,000 people, and its small defence force of sixty-eight Royal Marines was quickly overwhelmed by the South American invaders. The following day South Georgia, an even more remote island a further 800 miles (1,287 km) into the Atlantic, was also invaded. The twenty-two British marines stationed there put up a brave fight – even managing to down an Argentinian helicopter – but in the face of overwhelming numbers, they too were forced to surrender.

The British territories in the South Atlantic were British no more.

Ownership of the Falkland Islands had been a sore point with Argentina for over a century. Although variously claimed as a territory of France, Spain and Argentina throughout their history, in 1833 Britain took definitive control of the Islands, and they officially became a Crown Colony in 1840.

Argentina had never accepted Britain's rule over the Falklands. And now they had done something about it.

Eight thousand miles (12,874 km) north, Prime Minister Margaret Thatcher didn't care what the Argentinians thought. As far as Britain was concerned, the Falklands were part of the Crown, and would stay part of the Crown.

Approval for a task force to be sent to retake the islands was given the same day. The first submarine set sail from Scotland on 4 April; the first two aircraft carriers left Portsmouth twenty-four hours later. The whole force would eventually number 127 ships.

With them was a unit from 22 SAS, under the command of Lieutenant Colonel Michael Rose, who had masterminded the Iranian embassy rescue. They – along with sixty-seven men from the Special Boat Service – would have a crucial role to play in the coming conflict.

Initially at least, few people outside Britain believed the task force had any chance of retaking the islands. The huge distances involved, the harsh Antarctic conditions, as well as the superior number of men and strike aircraft available to the Argentinians, all weighed the odds firmly against the British – so much so that a US Navy assessment reportedly described success as 'a military impossibility'.

If Britain was to prove them wrong, it needed a boost, as soon as possible. The target: South Georgia.

Who dares wins.

◆ ◆ ◆

Operation Paraquet began life as a reconnaissance exercise. Units from the SAS and SBS were to covertly infiltrate South Georgia at two points: the SAS by helicopter on the northern glacier at Fortuna Bay, the SBS by dinghy at Hound Bay, to the south. Both would make their way towards the Argentine garrison at Grytviken, assessing troop numbers and positions along the way.

The SBS part of the operation achieved little. Hampered by bad luck and bad weather, they suffered damage to the dinghies early on and were forced to retreat back to the fleet without sighting any enemy troops.

The SAS fared even worse. Fifteen men led by Captain Gavin Hamilton had been dropped onto Fortuna Glacier on 21 April by two Wessex helicopters and immediately fell foul of the bitter Antarctic conditions. A force-ten storm had blown up: battered by 100-mile-per-hour (161-km) winds and with the temperature plummeting to twenty-five degrees below zero, the troopers were unable to make any progress across the exposed glacier. There was nothing to do but try to set up camp and wait out the storm.

Even that proved impossible. There was no hiding from the blizzard, and within minutes their tents had been whipped away by the wind. Hunkering down in whatever shelter they could find, huddled in crevices and behind rocks, with frostbite threatening to set in, Hamilton's men endured fifteen hours before the captain finally radioed back to the fleet. 'Unable to move. Environmental casualties imminent.'

Three helicopters were sent to rescue the team, but with conditions on the glacier now in full whiteout, one of the Wessex's span out of control and crashed. Mercifully, no one was hurt, and the men onboard were loaded onto the remaining two choppers. Again, the storm struck: a second helicopter crashed, though again, without sustaining any casualties.

Finally, after dropping its first load of men, the third Wessex managed to ferry the last of the SAS troopers back to HMS *Antrim*, the pilot barely controlling the overloaded craft to make an emergency landing on the deck.

So far, so dismal. Two helicopters lost, nothing gained ... though thankfully, a little frostbite aside, no casualties.

The following day, intelligence reported the approach of an Argentinian submarine, the *Santa Fe*, ferrying reinforcements for the island. The task force dispersed their ships, and drew up a new plan.

Under heavy cloud and a moonless sky, the *Santa Fe* docked at Grytviken, unloading fresh marines armed with anti-tank missiles. As it eased out of the bay again at first light on 25 April, the British were waiting.

Flying in low and fast out of the rising sun came the last remaining Wessex helicopter. As it swooped over the submarine it loosed two depth charges. The first was unlucky, bouncing off the hull and detonating harmlessly into the icy water.

The second did not miss. Exploding flush to the *Santa Fe*'s port side, it blew out a ballast tank and fatally damaged one of the submarine's fuel tanks. Crippled, leaking fuel and unable to dive, the vessel turned and limped back towards Grytviken, a sitting duck.

Behind the Wessex came further British firepower. Lynx and Wasp attack helicopters from HMS *Plymouth* and HMS *Brilliant* joined the assault, sending torpedoes and air-to-surface missiles screaming into the submarine. More damage, and the threat of a full hull breach. Somehow, the *Santa Fe* made it back to port ... but only just. As the garrison watched, her crew abandoned ship, and the British choppers wheeled away again, unharmed.

This was the chance. Major Guy Sheridan of the Royal Marines 42 Commando had been put in charge of any landing force. Without waiting for reinforcements, he now assembled what men he could – a scratch unit of seventy-nine marines, SAS and SBS troopers – and launched a full-scale assault on Grytviken.

The British soldiers took the garrison almost without firing a shot: dismayed by the destruction of their submarine and suddenly confronted by grim-faced special forces troops peeling out of helicopters with machine guns ready, the defenders lasted just fifteen minutes before surrendering.

The following day, the island's other garrison at Leith Harbour also capitulated. One hundred and fifty-five Argentinian soldiers had been captured, without a single British casualty.

More importantly, South Georgia had been liberated. A message was relayed back to Britain: 'Be pleased to inform Her Majesty that the White Ensign flies alongside the Union Jack in South Georgia. God save the Queen.'

PEBBLE ISLAND

FALKLAND ISLANDS, 14–15 MAY 1982

IN THE FREEZING early winter night, fourteen men moved silently across the stony, featureless terrain, crouching low, armed with mortars, grenade launchers and anti-tank rockets, and every other man carrying explosive charges. Their target: a hostile airfield, packed with deadly ground-attack planes and defended by a garrison of 150 enemy soldiers. Destroying the planes would give British forces a vital lift in the war, and clear the way for a counter-attack.

The skies were clear, the bright moonlight a mixed blessing: on the one hand the planes stood in stark relief to the black ground: sleek, bright targets impossible to miss. On the other, the commandos themselves were bathed in that same glow, their shadows – even running crouched double – stretching long behind them. One sentry had already been sighted on the approach; although they had managed to skirt around him without being noticed, the closer the British soldiers got to the runway, the flatter the ground became. Without cover, even the sloppiest of lookouts would surely spot them long before they could carry out their mission.

They were also racing against time. An operation that was planned as a ninety-minute raid had been curtailed into a thirty-minute smash-and-run attack. With weather conditions predicted to deteriorate rapidly, if they overran and missed their exit window, they'd be stuck here, outnumbered ten to one and with no hope of rescue.

The perimeter, or what passed for a perimeter, was unguarded, just as the earlier reconnaissance crew had promised. Without breaking stride, they were in and, splitting into seven two-man teams, raced across the airfield and got among the aircraft, explosives ready.

This wasn't David Stirling and Paddy Mayne lighting a fire under Rommel in the Libyan desert of 1941. This was forty years and 7,000 miles (11,265 km) later, on a windblown Argentinian-occupied island in the South Atlantic.

The SAS were about to play the oldest trick in their book.

◆ ◆ ◆

Pebble Island, just off the coast of West Falkland, held huge strategic importance for both sides in the conflict. The island itself was tiny – just 4 miles (6.5 km) across at its widest point and only 40 square miles (64 sq. km) in total, ordinarily home to barely two dozen people and several thousand sheep and penguins – but immediately after their invasion of the Falklands the Argentinians had established an airbase there. From Pebble Island they could command the skies over the entire archipelago – not only posing a constant threat to the British Task Force as a whole, but most tellingly, making any attempt to land a liberating force on the islands a far riskier and more costly proposition than British Command was prepared to chance.

For as long as planes could take off from Pebble Island, the Argentinians would control the Falklands. Something had to be done.

Step forward 'D' Squadron, 22 SAS.

Captain Gavin Hamilton, fresh from the trials of Fortuna Glacier and the liberation of South Georgia, volunteered his men for the job. It was to be a classic SAS manoeuvre, in every sense of the word. Just as with Stirling and Mayne's band of rogue heroes in the Western Desert four decades before, a small team would be dropped some miles from the airstrip, make their way under cover of darkness across enemy-occupied terrain, infiltrate the base, take out as many planes as they could, and then slip away again as all hell broke loose behind them, phantom terrors in the night.

First, it was vital to know exactly how many aircraft were at the base, as well as the positions and strength of the enemy based there.

On the evening of 10 May, eight men in four Klepper canoes – lightweight, low-profile, collapsible kayaks, the design of which had barely changed since SBS founder Roger Courtney first demonstrated their effectiveness – paddled silently into one of Pebble Island's myriad hidden coves.

The plan was to use the cover of darkness to yomp over the island's flat, featureless scrubland to Deep Fern Valley, where they could lay up and observe the airstrip. Rough seas and heavy winds delayed their approach, however, and by the time they had dismantled and packed up the kayaks and hiked to the recon spot, the skies were greying with dawn.

The team took the decision to dig in for the day, and wait out the nine hours of watery winter daylight.

As evening drew in, they found their reconnaissance spot and were soon radioing back their findings. There were eleven aircraft parked up at the base: four T-34C Turbo Mentor fighters, a Skyvan transport plane, and most importantly, six IA-58 Pucara ground-attack fighter-bombers. The Pucara was one of the Argentine Air Force's most potent weapons, armed with two 20-mm (0.8-inch) cannons and four machine guns, and capable of carrying bombs, rockets and even napalm. Putting the Pucaras out of action would be priority number one.

The SAS men also made careful note of the layout of the base. As well as the planes scattered across a large area around the runway – which was going to make getting to every one of them in time that much more difficult – there was also a barracks, fuel and ammo dumps and a watchtower at the far end of the strip. The team counted around 150 soldiers garrisoned there before they slipped away again into the last of the dark.

The reconnaissance mission had been a success, and Captain Hamilton had a plan. On the night of 14 May, fourteen of his men would be dropped by Sea King helicopters 4 miles (6.5 km) from the airstrip, where they would meet with the recon group. With them would be a support force of thirty troopers and an artillery spotter from 148 Commando.

As the strike team got in among the aircraft, the remaining men would act as a protection force, holding off the expected counter-attack from the Argentine garrison and pinning down the enemy long enough for the saboteurs to do their work. Meanwhile, the artillery spotter would direct supporting fire from the decks of HMS *Glamorgan*: the ship's guns would aim for the barracks, hoping to draw attention away from the real action.

Once the planes had been destroyed, the whole force was to withdraw to the waiting Sea Kings again, leaving only chaos and destruction behind them.

Captain Hamilton calculated that the raiders would need a ninety-minute offensive window for the operation to be carried out successfully. The helicopter pilots told him that would be an impossibility. The weather was deteriorating again; squalling headwinds and increasingly violent gusts meant it was going to take longer to fly in and out of the island than originally anticipated. After losing two Wessex choppers on South Georgia to the elements, they could not afford further mishaps, especially on such an important mission.

Hamilton was told his men would have just thirty minutes to do their worst to the Argentine airfield. He agreed: it would have to be enough.

◆ ◆ ◆

The strike force didn't waste any time once they reached the enemy base. As well as the mortar bombs and explosive charges, each man carried an M16 rifle, roughly half of which were fitted with underslung grenade launchers.

Their approach had so far gone undetected, but it was surely only a matter of time before a sentry or stray pair of eyes noticed the unfamiliar figures lurking in the moonlight. And with every minute vital, they simply did not have the luxury of executing a stealthier approach. Breaking cover, the two-man teams ran full-tilt at their targets, the bright full moon illuminating the entire base like daylight.

The Turbo Mentors were the easiest targets – the small single-engine planes were low enough to the ground for a man to make the leap onto the wing with a single bound – but the bigger, heavier Pucaras were a different prospect. Quickly, the raiders discovered the easiest way up onto the fuselage was for one man to give the other a 'leg-up' on to the wing, and then for that man to lean over to haul his partner up.

Another trick learned from Stirling and Mayne's adventures in the desert: each of the commandos placed his explosive charges in the same area of the planes – thereby ensuring that damaged craft couldn't be cannibalized for spare parts to rebuild other planes.

As well as setting the explosives, the commandos ripped out whatever cables and cockpit instruments they could, and, finally abandoning any idea of secrecy altogether, shot at the fuel tanks with their M16s.

As alarms rang, they let rip with the grenades and mortars, retreating back to their covering force at the perimeter and blowing the charges behind them.

Five planes exploded spectacularly, and the commandos trained their fire on the remaining six aircraft, raking the planes with grenade launchers and 66-mm (2.6-inch) LAW anti-tank rockets. This was the cue for the artillery spotter, and under his instruction, an incoming barrage of shells from HMS *Glamorgan* materialized from the blackness out to sea and tore into the garrison buildings.

If the airstrip had been bathed in quiet moonlight a few minutes before, now it was a vivid riot of colour and noise. Flames had engulfed most of the aircraft; further explosions came fast and erratically, each sending fireballs into the sky. The rattle of small-arms fire was punctuated by periodic whistles of tracers from the *Glamorgan*, booms of grenades going off, thuds from the mortars, and under it all the background crashes and groans of twisted and falling metal.

All at once there was a deafening new sound, and a flash brighter than any before: the *Glamorgan* had scored a direct hit on the airstrip's ammunition dump, the whole store going up in a mighty conflagration.

The SAS beat a retreat, continuing to fire until they were satisfied nobody was coming after them, making the Sea Kings with just minutes to spare. One man had a shrapnel wound, otherwise all were unscathed.

The response from the 150 Argentine soldiers stationed at the base had been minimal. Whether confused, disoriented, suffering from poor leadership, under the illusion they were experiencing a full-scale invasion, or simply just too terrified to fight back, they had barely engaged the SAS raiders at all.

At first light, as columns of thick, black smoke continued to rise from the blasted airfield, airborne reconnaissance gave its report.

The raid had been an unqualified success. In just thirty devastating minutes, the SAS team had completely destroyed all eleven aircraft at the base, including the six Pucaras. In addition, shells from the *Glamorgan* had obliterated the ammunition and fuel dumps, and one Argentine commander had been killed. The airfield at Pebble Island had been rendered useless, and half of the Argentine Air Force's entire number of Pucara attack planes taken out of the war altogether. Captain Gavin Hamilton and his partner in the raid had accounted for four of the Pucaras alone.

Paddy Mayne himself would have been proud.

BATTLE OF MOUNT KENT

FALKLAND ISLANDS, MAY–JUNE 1982

THE VOICE ON the radio was low and urgent, he spoke quickly and he wasn't wasting words, stating simply: 'We are in trouble.'

The radio operator was part of the Argentine special forces unit 602 Commando. The day before, the main body of his company had clashed with SAS troopers from 'D' Squadron and come off the worse, despite having superior numbers. Now, as a twelve-man patrol known as the 'Assault Section' had attempted to secure another position, they had been ambushed by the SAS. The fighting was fierce and prolonged, and once again, the Argentines were struggling.

Forty minutes later, another message: 'There are English all around us ... you had better hurry up.'

From that point on, the radio was silent.

During the last days of May 1982, the opposing British and Argentine elite units engaged in direct battle with each other for the first time. Historians remain divided, but for many it also marks the first time two special forces units of any country had fought in direct combat against each other.

The prize: Mount Kent, a 1,093-foot peak overlooking the Falklands' capital Port Stanley and a vital strategic stronghold from which to control any attempt to liberate the island. Argentine forces held the capital; the British, fresh from securing a beachhead at San Carlos Bay on the north-west coast of East Falkland, and then winning a significant victory at Goose Green, were closing in on what would surely be the decisive battle for the Falklands.

But the Argentines were not defeated yet, and in the special forces units of 601 and 602 Commando they had two highly capable squadrons with the experience and ability to cause serious damage to the British army. Once again, the commanders looked to the SAS to clear a path for them.

◆ ◆ ◆

Captain Gavin Hamilton, the twenty-nine-year-old squadron leader who had shown his qualities on the frozen wastes of Fortuna Glacier and led the destruction of Pebble Island airstrip, once more stepped up to the plate.

The men of 'D' Squadron were to be tasked with taking Mount Kent. With no idea of what enemy positions might be entrenched on the slopes, a full-on assault was never an option, so on 25 May an initial reconnaissance patrol under the command of Major Cedric Delves was despatched to the mountain. They reported that although the majority of the Argentine force had left the area – either redeployed to Goose Green or moved back to the next two peaks, Mount Two Sisters and Mount Harriet – there nevertheless remained a significant special forces presence in the area.

On 27 May, Hamilton's men joined them: their job was to engage the 601 and 602 Commando units on the mountain, and hold the ground until the main force of the Paras and Royal Marines could catch up and reinforce the position.

The first encounter between the two special forces units would come two nights later.

Forty men from 602 Commando surprised an SAS patrol on the slopes of the mountain – as both sides scrambled for cover and position, a tense and drawn-out battle ensued. The British men may have been the best-trained elite unit in the world, but the Argentine commandos were disciplined, motivated, held superior numbers, and, crucially, were more at home in the barren, icy conditions. It was a close-run thing, but eventually the SAS gained the upper hand and the Argentines withdrew. The tally: two British wounded, and one Argentine casualty.

The following day, twelve men from the same Argentinian unit attempted to take a defensive position on Bluff Cove Peak – and this time it was their turn to be ambushed. Waiting for them were fifteen SAS troopers. The men from the Assault Section fought a fierce defence, but even as their radio operator sent his desperate calls for reinforcements ('We are in trouble ... There are English all around us'), they once again were forced to withdraw. This time, the tally was two Argentine dead, two British wounded.

The deadly game of cat and mouse continued, with multiple encounters over the following days. Captain Hamilton led another successful ambush in which four enemy commandos were captured; a separate raid on an Argentine position at Top Malo House, just west of Mount Kent, saw further British success.

Gradually, led by Major Delves and Captain Harrison, the SAS men prevailed, driving the enemy slowly eastwards, until finally, on 11 June, the area was decisively won with the arrival of the main force of Royal Marines and Parachute battalions of 3 Commando Brigade. Five British troopers had been killed in the running battles, and a further eleven wounded; the Argentine special forces had lost twice that number, as well as another five taken prisoner.

Brigadier Julian Thompson, who commanded 3 Commando Brigade, later attributed the successful captures of the mountains west of Port Stanley – and the subsequent liberation of the capital itself on 14 June – in large part to the SAS operation on Mount Kent. Without Captain Harrison and Major Delves' bravery, he wrote, the Argentine special forces units 'would have had a turkey shoot on the vulnerable helicopters and the troops as they jumped out, temporarily disoriented in the darkness; the operation would have been a disaster'.

For his part in the operation, Major Delves was awarded the Distinguished Service Order.

◆ ◆ ◆

There is a tragic postscript to the story, however. Captain Gavin Hamilton had been redeployed from Mount Kent on 5 June to lead a four-man observation patrol on the neighbouring island of West Falkland. Operating deep behind enemy lines, he successfully established a reconnaissance position on the high ground overlooking the town of Port Howard, the island's largest settlement and main Argentinian stronghold on West Falkland.

For five days they stayed entrenched above the town on a ridge called Many Branch Point, relaying vital and detailed intelligence on enemy troop numbers and movements back to the task force, until, on 10 June, their luck ran out.

As Hamilton and signaller Corporal Roy Fonseka ventured forward from their base on another recon mission, they stumbled into a patrol from 601 Commando. A furious exchange of fire began, with the SAS men all too aware that barely 2,000 metres (2,187 yards) below them lay the entire Argentine garrison at Port Howard.

Holding the position meant it would only be a matter of time before enemy reinforcements arrived, and with there being no sign that the other two men back at Many Bridge Point were even aware of the fighting, Hamilton signalled to Fonseka to fall back. The two men would beat a fighting retreat, with Hamilton providing covering fire for his signaller.

The captain had already taken one bullet in the arm early in the fight; nevertheless, he squared his jaw and unleashed a stream of automatic fire towards the enemy commandos as Fonseka withdrew, pinning the Argentines down, drawing their fire towards him.

It was a typically brave move, and it nearly paid off. Satisfied Fonseka had withdrawn far enough, Hamilton attempted to follow his corporal ... and took a second bullet square on. He was killed instantly.

Just four days later the Argentinians surrendered. The Falkland Islands had been liberated after seventy-four days of occupation, and Captain Gavin Hamilton had played a key role in three of the most important SAS operations of the war – in South Georgia, at Pebble Island, and on the slopes of Mount Kent. The Argentine Commander of Port Howard, Colonel Juan Ramon Mabragana, later told British forces that Hamilton was 'the most courageous man I have ever seen'.

In October 1982, he was posthumously awarded the Military Cross. The citation concluded: 'Captain Hamilton displayed outstanding determination and an extraordinary will to continue the fight in spite of being confronted by hopeless odds and being wounded. He furthermore showed supreme courage and sense of duty by his conscious decision to sacrifice himself on behalf of his signaller. His final, brave and unselfish act will be an inspiration to all who follow in the SAS.'

OPERATION JUDY

N. IRELAND, 8 MAY 1987

AS THE SUN SET on a May evening in 1987 in County Armagh, Northern Ireland, the sleepy calm of the village of Loughall was shattered by a squeal of tyres and roar of engines. A huge backhoe loader was smashing through the security fence surrounding the village police station; accelerating through the breach behind it was a blue Toyota van. The vehicles held eight members of the Provisional IRA, dressed in blue boilersuits and balaclavas, wielding automatic assault rifles, a shotgun and a revolver. In the bucket of the loader was an oil drum containing around 350 pounds (159 kg) of Semtex.

As the digger crunched over the wreckage of the fence and continued towards the station, the van overtook it, screeching to a stop close by. Three men jumped from the digger, two leaning into the bucket to light fuses, and along with their five colleagues from the van, ran towards the station, guns cocked.

Forty seconds later the bomb detonated. Metal and masonry flew, and at the same time, the IRA men unloaded their weapons into the building.

If they felt any jubilation, it was short-lived. Within seconds of the explosion, their fire was returned, with interest. The SAS had been waiting.

◆ ◆ ◆

Since the events of Bloody Sunday in January 1972, when British soldiers shot twenty-six unarmed Catholic civilians during a protest in Derry, Northern Ireland, killing thirteen of them outright, the relationship between the British security forces and the Provisional Irish Republican Army (or IRA) had deteriorated, apparently irreparably. By the late 1980s, as far as the IRA were concerned, they were in a state of war with the British – and with anyone they deemed to be furthering or supporting British interests in Northern Ireland.

It would not be until the Good Friday Agreement of 1998 that the conflict between the largely Protestant Unionists, who wanted Northern Ireland to remain part of the United Kingdom, and the mostly Catholic Republicans, who were in favour of a united, single-state Ireland, finally came to an end.

Until then, deep civil unrest. Paramilitary groups were formed on both sides, and for two decades the Troubles, as the unofficial war was known, spawned countless acts of terrorism, with bombings, shootings, kidnappings and beatings horrifyingly commonplace.

Although the Unionists and Republicans were supposedly fighting against each other, it was a messy, chaotic conflict, with many innocent civilians falling victim to the violence – sometimes accidentally, sometimes by design. Caught in the thick of it, ostensibly as peacekeepers, were the British army, deployed to the province after the government concluded that the Northern Irish security forces simply could not cope alone. Whether the presence of British soldiers on the streets of cities like Belfast and Derry helped or actually made the problem worse remains a subject of fierce debate among historians and politicians to this day.

Away from the big cities, the violence was less visible, but that didn't mean it wasn't there. And in the mostly rural counties of Tyrone and Armagh on the southern border, pro-Republican feelings ran strong.

The East Tyrone Brigade was one of the IRA's most active, most violent and most committed paramilitary groups. Even before Bloody Sunday, they had claimed their first British soldier, when John Rudman, a twenty-one-year-old with the Light Infantry, was shot dead in an ambush in September 1971.

By the mid-1980s they were striking across Tyrone and neighbouring Armagh in a concerted campaign against the province's police force, the Royal Ulster Constabulary, who they saw as part of the British 'invaders' of Ireland. Among their attacks was one on The Birches RUC base in County Armagh, for which the Brigade pioneered the use of a backhoe loader to breach the security fence. Now they planned to use the same tactic on the station at Loughgall.

The attack was timed to coincide with the station's three RUC officers closing up for the day – it seems the idea was to destroy both the station and the policemen manning it.

What the IRA didn't know was that British intelligence had already got wind of the plan.

◆ ◆ ◆

In the hours before the attack, the base was secretly evacuated, and a team of twenty-four SAS troopers, as well as members of the RUC's specialist Mobile Support Unit, took up positions in and around the station. Six SAS men along with the RUC were inside the building; the remaining eighteen hid in five other locations, covering the approach to and exit from the station. All were armed with M16 and L7A2 automatic machine guns.

Right on cue, shortly before 19.00 hours, the digger was spotted trundling through the quiet country roads towards Loughgall, the bomb in the bucket hidden under a pile of rubble. Behind it came the van. The SAS team watched as both vehicles made a slow pass of the station, the men inside scanning for evidence of an ambush or trap. The troopers stayed calm, regulating their breathing, slowing their pulses. Nobody would move until the signal came.

Finally, the digger rolled towards the perimeter fence and paused, engine idling. Two men sprang from the van, pulling balaclavas over their faces, weapons already drawn. One climbed each side of the bucket, cigarette lighters in their free hands.

The throttle was engaged, the loader lurched forward, the fence buckled under its weight, the van accelerated and swerved around it, the fuses were lit, the men jumped out of both vehicles, and the attack was on.

The sudden deafening crash of the bomb tore through the evening air, the blast mangling the digger, smashing the station windows, sending glass and metal and rubble flying ... and adding to the cacophony came the rattle of the paramilitary men's guns as they targeted the building.

Immediately, their gunfire was drowned out by a swift, concentrated and deadly hail of bullets in reply. The attackers were exactly where the waiting SAS wanted them – caught in the crossfire of a classic 'D' formation ambush, they didn't stand a chance.

Over 600 rounds of ammunition were offloaded in just seconds. As those men who weren't immediately cut down scrambled for cover behind the van, SAS troopers concentrated their fire on the vehicle itself, riddling it with more than 125 bullet holes.

Amid the carnage a third vehicle appeared. Inside were two men in blue overalls, and, believing them to be more IRA fighters, SAS troopers outside the station opened fire on the car from behind. The driver, Anthony Hughes, was killed instantly; the passenger, his brother Oliver, managed to jump out of the car before he too was shot fourteen times.

Somehow, he survived – and it was later established that neither brother was involved in the attack at all, but tragically happened to be in the wrong place at the wrong time.

Meanwhile, a kind of calm had descended. As the SAS moved to secure the scene outside the station – broken glass, rubble and spent cartridges littering the ground like gruesome confetti – it quickly became obvious that not a single one of the attackers had survived the storm of bullets.

All eight members of the East Tyrone Brigade had been killed in the fight. It was the IRA's largest loss of life in a single incident in the history of the Troubles. In reply, one SAS trooper had minor facial injuries, and the two RUC men sustained non-life-threatening head injuries in the explosion.

Operation Judy had been a success for the SAS, but not without cost, or controversy. The killing of innocent civilian Anthony Hughes and the shooting of his brother Oliver resulted in a later apology from the British government and an undisclosed out-of-court settlement to Anthony's widow.

Meanwhile, the IRA seized upon the incident as another example of British oppression, with supporters of the organization dubbing the eight men the 'Loughgall Martyrs', and thousands attending their funerals.

It would be another eleven long years before the Good Friday Agreement was signed, and the attack on Loughgall would not be the last action the SAS saw in Northern Ireland – nor the last time they came up against the paramilitaries of East Tyrone.

OPERATION FLAVIUS

GIBRALTAR, 6 MARCH 1988

IN PURSUIT OF ITS GOAL of a united Ireland, the Provisional IRA was not averse to taking its self-styled 'war' to other British territories, and in late 1987, MI5 began to suspect that the IRA could be planning an attack in Gibraltar, the British-dependent territory on the southern tip of Spain. Spanish police had begun monitoring the activities of several known IRA operatives regularly travelling from Belfast to the Costa del Sol under false identities, and were concerned that the paramilitaries had set up a dedicated cell in the area. By February 1988 intelligence confirmed that the target was to be the changing of the guard ceremony outside the Governor's Residence in the old town; the method, a car packed with explosives, to be detonated remotely.

The Gibraltar authorities requested special assistance from the British government – and the SAS were given the task of intercepting the IRA cell and stopping the bomb ... by deadly force, if necessary. The operation was given the codename Flavius.

Two men – Danny McCann and Seán Savage – and a woman – Mairéad Farrell – were quickly identified as the likeliest persons to carry out the attack. They were well known to intelligence as senior activists in the IRA specializing in explosives: both McCann and Farrell had already served prison sentences. By early 1988 all were making regular trips to southern Spain under false identities.

At the end of February, the three once again travelled to Malaga on the Costa del Sol, some 90 miles (145 km) from Gibraltar; this time the SAS followed them. Seven troopers were assigned to the 'hit' team charged with apprehending the IRA operatives – in order to protect their identities, they have never been officially named, but only subsequently identified as Soldiers A to G.

Although the British special forces unit had direct authority from the government – with some sources claiming that Prime Minister Margaret Thatcher herself gave personal approval to Operation Flavius – they nevertheless had to tread something of a diplomatic tightrope.

The existence of the British-dependent territory of Gibraltar on the Spanish mainland had long been a source of tension between the British and Spanish authorities; it seemed an anachronistic and outdated relic of the Empire to most Spaniards – a view the IRA themselves could perhaps sympathize with. The idea of British special forces men operating in the region was then, to say the least, an uncomfortable prospect for the Spanish government.

Officially, the SAS were there purely to assist the Gibraltar police in arresting the suspects. They needed their authorization to act, and even then could do so only if the IRA personnel were positively identified parking a bomb-loaded car and then attempting to cross the border back to Spain.

On the other hand, the British government was painfully aware of a similar IRA atrocity committed at the Northern Irish town of Enniskillen just four months earlier, when a bomb was detonated near the town's war memorial during a Remembrance Day parade. The IRA insisted later that its intended target had been the British soldiers attending the parade, but the harsh facts were that ten civilians and one police officer had been killed, with a further sixty-three, mostly elderly, people injured.

Another Enniskillen – especially in a politically sensitive area like Gibraltar – had to be avoided at all costs.

◆ ◆ ◆

At lunchtime on 6 March 1988, Seán Savage crossed the border from Spain to Gibraltar in a white Renault 5 car, and parked up close to the Governor's Residence, and the square used for the changing of the guard ceremony.

To Savage's eyes at least, nothing about the square that afternoon seemed unusual. Far from being enclosed behind high walls and security gates, the Governor's Residence, a grand sixteenth-century former Franciscan monastery known as The Convent, stood in the heart of the old town. As Savage surveyed the scene, the area was bustling with people strolling, eating, drinking, or simply enjoying the ambience of a warm Sunday afternoon in Gibraltar.

What he did not know was that hidden among those people were MI5 operatives, undercover Gibraltar police officers, and SAS troopers in plain clothes carrying 9-mm Browning Hi-Power pistols concealed under their jackets.

All watched him park the Renault, and all watched as he was approached by Danny McCann and Mairéad Farrell. The three appeared to check the car, and then at 14.50 hours, they strolled away.

Immediately once they were out of eyesight, an explosives expert from the SAS team moved to examine the car. Although there were none of the obvious signs of a bomb – no suspicious wires or antennae, no depressed axles that might indicate a heavy weight in the boot – he reported back that the aerial for the radio did look odd, and that the boot could nonetheless be loaded with a more lightweight plastic explosive such as Semtex. He couldn't say for sure there was a bomb in the car, but he also couldn't say for sure there wasn't.

As McCann, Savage and Farrell continued to walk north, the SAS, MI5 and Gibraltar police debated what to do. They could not be definitively certain that the Renault contained a bomb, but what was beyond question was that three known and identified senior IRA operatives had crossed into Gibraltar and left a hired car in the area of the planned changing of the guard, just as intelligence had warned.

Gibraltar Police Commissioner Joseph Canepa made the call. The three suspects had to be arrested.

At 15.40 hours, he officially signed over control of the operation to the SAS. Two minutes later, the order was given to apprehend the operatives.

By this time, all three were a mile (1.6 km) north of their abandoned car and moving along Winston Churchill Avenue, the main thoroughfare to the Spanish border. The four SAS men who had been following them quickened their pace, closing the distance, preparing for the takedown – according to protocol, peacefully if at all possible, but otherwise by whatever means necessary to preserve innocent life. If one of the IRA members had a remote trigger for the car bomb, and was to activate it, the results could be catastrophic.

Either spooked by the movement behind them or else by prearranged design, Savage suddenly split from his colleagues and, turning around, doubled back south, the way he had come, walking right by one of the SAS troopers as he did so.

The trooper ignored him, and along with one other man, continued following McCann and Farrell; as he did so, the other two SAS soldiers peeled off to tail Savage.

The distance between the SAS and each of the three IRA members closed, and then, as one of the SAS team later testified, 'events overtook' them.

A police car, called towards the Governor's Residence for the anticipated questioning of the suspects was at that moment passing the exact same spot on Winston Churchill Avenue. Attempting to move faster through the traffic, the driver switched his siren on; the sudden noise spooked McCann and Farrell just as the SAS were about to move in. Stopping in their tracks they turned – and were confronted by their pursuers.

For a second, Mairéad Farrell stared at the SAS trooper square in the eye. As he drew his pistol and began to shout a warning, Danny McCann made what was later described as an 'aggressive movement' across his body. Not knowing if he was reaching for a weapon or a remote detonator, the trooper opened fire, felling him with a single shot to the back.

Now it was Farrell's turn to react. A movement was made towards her handbag – again, uncertain what she was reaching for, the trooper shot. As she fell, the second SAS man fired into the now-prone bodies of both IRA members. McCann was hit a total of five times, Farrell six.

As the shots rang out, Savage, who had quickened his pace southwards, spun around, directly into the path of the other two SAS men. One called out a warning, but as Savage reached towards his jacket pocket, both opened fire. Between them, the two troopers put fifteen bullets into him.

The whole encounter took just seconds.

All three IRA operatives were dead, no civilians were hurt, and no bomb had detonated. Operation Flavius appeared to have been a success – and prevented what could have been another Enniskillen-level atrocity.

◆ ◆ ◆

The congratulations were short-lived.

Examination of the three dead suspects revealed that not only were they all unarmed, but also none of them were carrying a remote bomb trigger. When Savage's Renault was safely removed and taken apart by bomb disposal experts it was also found to contain no explosives.

What had been a triumph was now a potential disaster – and the IRA themselves were not slow to react, describing the operation as a cold-blooded execution of unarmed suspects by a trigger-happy British army who had always intended to assassinate their victims.

An official inquest was launched, hearing evidence from seventy-nine witnesses including the SAS personnel involved, as well as Gibraltar police and civilians. After nearly a month, the jury returned a verdict of 'lawful killing'.

Two years later, the families of McCann, Savage and Farrell took their case to the European Court of Human Rights; although the court found that the British government had violated Article 2 of the Convention (which covers the 'right to life' – meaning that nobody, including the government, can lawfully try to end someone's life), they also rejected the families' claim for damages, ruling that all three victims had been killed while preparing an act of terrorism.

Another car was later found close to the IRA cell's base on the Costa del Sol, containing a large amount of Semtex, along with detonators, timers and 200 rounds of ammunition. The keys were on Farrell's person when she was shot.

The most controversial SAS operation of the Troubles – and an incident described by the Gibraltar police as 'the most violent event' in the history of that force – continues to provoke fierce debate to this day. It highlights the split-second, do-or-die pressures those serving in the SAS face every time they are called into action.

BRAVO TWO ZERO

IRAQ, JANUARY 1991

THE SAS'S MOST FAMOUS post-war mission is arguably also its most fiercely contested. Contrasting accounts of those involved in the operation have made it almost impossible to say definitively what happened. Only the men who were there and survived know the truth ... and they don't always agree on what the truth was.

Whichever version you believe, some things remain indisputable, however. That the Bravo Two Zero patrol deep behind enemy lines in the Iraq War was a disaster is beyond doubt; but so too is the bravery and determination of the men involved. It is celebrated not because it was an example of the SAS's superiority on the battlefield, but because it is a testament to the mettle of the men who make up the elite force.

◆ ◆ ◆

In January 1991, the SAS were once again in the desert. The response to Iraqi dictator Saddam Hussein's invasion of Kuwait the previous August had been instant and uncompromising: a coalition of thirty-five countries had come together, spearheaded by the US and the British, to liberate Kuwait and impose sanctions and a demilitarized zone on Iraq. Thirty years later, history records that the Western Allies' victory was swift, but for those on the ground, the reality of fighting in such a vast and hostile environment against a motivated and often-fanatical enemy was anything but easy.

For none more so than the SAS. Amid the huge air and naval bombardment, the special forces unit was tasked with dangerous, top-secret undercover missions deep into Iraq itself. These did not always go to plan.

On 22 January, an eight-man patrol from 'B' Squadron, 22 SAS based in Saudi Arabia was lifted by Chinook helicopter and dropped into the Iraqi desert. Led by Sergeant Steven Mitchell, later to become famous under the pen-name Andy McNab, the team also included Corporal Colin Armstrong, who also wrote about the mission as Chris Ryan. They were given the name 'Bravo Two Zero', after their radio call sign.

The team's mission was to penetrate the area along the main supply route from the capital Baghdad to north-west Iraq, where they would set up an observation post, monitor enemy movements, report back intelligence and locate and if possible destroy Scud missile launchers.

Whether through bad luck, bad planning, bad preparation or bad decision-making, things began to go wrong from the moment the troopers touched down. Almost immediately after landing, the patrol radio developed a fault: they could still transmit messages, but from that point on would not be able to receive any.

Nevertheless, the SAS did what the SAS always do. They adapted and improvised to meet the changing circumstances. Shouldering their packs, they pressed on into the desert.

As it turned out, the faulty radio was to be the least of their problems. According to Ryan, the team were woefully unprepared for the conditions in the desert: they had not been briefed properly on the weather or the terrain, had been issued with Second World War-era maps, and were wearing battledress unsuitable for the freezing January nights on the exposed desert floor, when the temperature regularly dropped below zero.

The following day things got worse. The men had hiked to their planned observation post and set up a makeshift base from which to monitor troop and missile movements, but late in the afternoon a shepherd stumbled upon their position, soon followed by a tractor and other vehicles. With the site clearly unsuitable as an observation post and their position compromised, the patrol had to move – and concerned that the area could soon be swarming with hostile forces, the decision was made to sacrifice equipment for speed: all non-essential gear was abandoned and the eight men set off at pace.

Following standard operating procedure, the patrol retraced their steps to their original infiltration point, where a helicopter was scheduled to land briefly once every twenty-four hours in case of such an emergency. Unable to receive messages on the malfunctioning radio, they could do nothing but wait and hope.

They waited in vain. More bad luck: at precisely the period that the helicopter would have rendezvoused with the team, the pilot was suffering from an illness. He abandoned the flight, and what should have been an easy pickup was missed.

With no way of knowing the real reason for the helicopter's absence, the patrol assumed the worst. No exfiltration team was coming, today or any other day. They were alone in the desert hundreds of miles from friendly lines and if they were to get out again it seemed they would have to do it by themselves, so they shouldered their packs and set off on foot, north-west towards the

Syrian border, with some 200 miles (322 km) of barren wasteland and the whole Iraqi army ahead of them.

It was to be the hardest march of their lives. Conditions in the desert were appalling. Cover was sparse, the landscape a vast, arid plain of hard bedrock broken up by wadis, ridges and depressions. Crossing such terrain was exceptionally hard-going, but doing so while trying to remain undetected, doubly so. In addition, the weather was proving to be as great a danger as the threat of Iraqi patrols. As the sun set, the mercury plummeted, and the obsolete battledress the troopers wore gave little warmth.

On the following night, the cold began to tell. One of the men, Sergeant Vincent Phillips, had begun displaying signs of hypothermia the day before – as they marched on through the freezing darkness, his symptoms worsened. Dizzy, delirious, hallucinating and unable to keep up with the others, he became separated from the team, stumbling away into the ink-black desert alone.

By the time his absence was noted, it was already too late. Sergeant Phillips would later be noted as the first fatality of Bravo Two Zero, killed by the cold.

As they searched in vain for him, more misfortune: in the darkness and confusion the entire patrol became fatally separated. The eight men were now seven, and split into two groups, with Ryan and Trooper Malcolm McGown cut off from the others.

Continuing to press north-west, both parties quickly ran into trouble: such was the local, often fanatical, hostility to Western soldiers that it was not only enemy troops that the SAS had to worry about – armed civilians would fire on sight, and even those who didn't have guns would attack them with whatever they could bring to hand. It was one skirmish after another.

Just four days after their insertion into the desert, McNab's group of five were reduced to three. One man, Trooper Robert Consiglio, was shot and killed by civilian militia as he desperately defended his team's position; his colleague, Trooper Steven Lane, became a second victim of hypothermia, overcome after swimming across a river to escape another ambush.

The remaining three commandos were finally captured, after a heroic last stand.

◆ ◆ ◆

According to McNab, he, along with Lance Corporal Ian Pring and Trooper Mike Coburn, were moved between a succession of prisons over the following weeks, where, after being joined by Trooper Malcolm McGown, who had also been captured after killing several enemy soldiers in a last-ditch firefight, they spent the next six weeks suffering horrific torture at the hands of their captors.

Of the last man in the patrol, Corporal Colin Armstrong (better known now as Chris Ryan), there was no word.

For a month and a half the SAS men were beaten and abused by Iraqi interrogators desperate to know who they were and what was the purpose of their mission so deep into Iraq. Stripped naked and trussed up, they had teeth smashed and wrenched out with pliers, bones broken and left unset, cigarettes stubbed out on their skin and burning metal spoons seared onto their flesh. On one occasion, McNab says they were paraded through the streets to roaring crowds of men, women and children hurling stones, punching and scratching at them, before being taken back to the notorious Abu Ghraib prison and beaten with wooden paddles and a metal rod with a heavy ball on the end until they passed out with pain. On another, he was forced to clear a blocked toilet with his bare hands – and then lick them clean.

The men were given little food and barely any water. Suffering from dehydration and diarrhoea, in excruciating agony from their injuries and denied any medical care, they were made to sleep in their own filth, any hours of rest they could manage being their only respite from the daily interrogations and torture.

Throughout their ordeal, every one of the SAS men remained true to the regiment. None revealed who they were, or what the purpose of their mission was. Eventually, on 5 March, four days after the Western victory and official ceasefire, all four were released, broken, maimed ... but alive.

Only one man had evaded torture, or death in the desert.

After Trooper McGown had been captured, Chris Ryan had managed to escape, and as the last man standing from Bravo Two Zero patrol, he began an extraordinary 190-mile (305-km) solo march across Iraq to the Syrian border.

For seven days and eight nights he made his way north, covering upwards of 25 miles (40 km) every twenty-four hours. What little food rations were left ran out almost immediately, and for the last three days of his march, he survived on just a few drops of water – at one stage, the thirst became so bad he drank polluted water from a chemical plant, burning the inside of his mouth and throat.

By the time Ryan reached the border he was barely conscious, hallucinating, and suffering from hypothermia. He had lost over two stone in weight, his feet were bleeding and his toenails had fallen off, and there was severe damage to several of his internal organs, including his liver. His 190-mile (305-km) hike remains the longest escape through enemy territory of any British soldier.

Bravo Two Zero patrol had been a disaster. The patrol had failed to achieve any of its aims, had lost two troopers to the cold and a third to enemy fire, and four of the remaining five commandos suffered unspeakable horrors at the hands of the torturers of Abu Ghraib.

And yet, by simply enduring, those men became heroes. Accounts of the action by Andy McNab and Chris Ryan have become international bestsellers and made their authors household names.

The true mettle of an SAS man is not always the number of enemy killed or equipment destroyed, but courage and resilience in the face of unimaginable adversity. It's not about how many times you get knocked down, but how many times you get back up again.

CLONOE AMBUSH

N. IRELAND, 16 FEBRUARY 1992

AT A LITTLE AFTER 22.30 hours on 16 February 1992, the quiet streets of Coalisland, a former coal-mining village near Lough Neagh in County Tyrone, Northern Ireland, rumbled with an unfamiliar sound. A heavy lorry hurtled through the town; on its back was mounted a massive Soviet-era anti-aircraft weapon. Another car followed. The drivers and passengers all wore balaclavas, some carried Kalashnikov assault rifles.

At that time on a Sunday evening most of the residents of Coalisland were either asleep or preparing for bed, and as the two vehicles roared to a stop outside the RUC base in the centre of the village, the streets were deserted.

The sleepy peace did not last for long. Yelling and cheering, passengers spilled from the car and began shooting at the police station, while another man brought the lorry's heavy machine gun to bear. Bright tracer fire screamed through the night, armour-piercing ammunition slamming into the building, pulverizing brick and cement like cardboard.

After just a few minutes the base had been reduced to little more than rubble. Still shouting, the men unfurled an Irish tricolour over the back of the lorry, and, headlights and hazard lights flashing, drove off again, leaving what was left of the building smoking behind them. The East Tyrone Brigade were back.

◆ ◆ ◆

In the five years since the ambush at Loughgall, the East Tyrone branch of the Provisional IRA had only redoubled its campaign of terror against the British in Northern Ireland. Far from being cowed by the loss of eight of its most senior operatives, it instead increased its activities in the province. Between 1987 and 1992 the Brigade attacked nearly 100 military and police facilities, seriously damaging thirty-three of them, as well as killing eleven people in Tyrone and Armagh and downing a Gazelle helicopter near the Tyrone village of Augher.

In response, twenty-eight members of the East Tyrone Brigade had been killed over the same period, all at the hands of British forces. To say there was bad blood between the two would be an understatement.

In February 1992, British intelligence learned of another planned attack, this time on the RUC base at Coalisland. Just as had happened at Loughgall, this time the SAS would be waiting.

Unlike in the ambush at Loughgall, however, the SAS could not engage the IRA men in a direct firefight as they attacked. Intelligence reported that, rather than detonate a bomb by the police station, they were planning instead to utilize a huge DShK heavy machine gun. Getting into a shootout with the DShK would not be a good idea: the Second World War anti-aircraft weapon fired armour-piercing tracers, and the potential collateral damage to neighbouring property and civilians – not to mention the risk to the soldiers themselves – could be catastrophic.

Instead, the SAS would wait until after the attack on the

unmanned base had been completed, and the gun dismantled. This plan also had the advantage of giving the IRA shooters a false sense of confidence; thinking they had got away with another successful demolition of a police station, they would be less alert to any ambush.

◆ ◆ ◆

As the four IRA men sped away from the ruined RUC station at Coalisland, they weren't taking any pains to hide their movements – on the contrary, they behaved as if they wanted the whole province to see them. This wasn't a quick, discreet getaway, so much as a full-blown victory parade. The drivers kept their orange hazard lights on, the man with the heavy gun on the back of the lorry waved his flag, and as they passed the former home of IRA member Tony Dorris, who had recently been killed by the British army, they leaned out of their vehicles, shooting noisy volleys from their Kalashnikovs in the air and shouting, 'Up the 'RA! That's for Tony Dorris!'

The carnival atmosphere continued all the way to their planned getaway point, 2 miles (3.2 km) from Coalisland, in the even-smaller village of Clonoe. Pulling into the car park of St Patrick's Catholic Church, the men abandoned the vehicles and prepared to transfer to two fresh cars, complete with new drivers. First, the DHsK had to be dismounted – there was no way the paramilitaries were going to leave such prized ordnance behind.

Hidden behind the walls of the church car park, the SAS watched and waited.

The moment the heavy gun was no longer a threat, they struck. Tight bursts of automatic gunfire tore out of the darkness, striking down three of the men in seconds. Two of them, Peter Clancy and Kevin O'Donnell, were killed while still dismantling the DHsK – Clancy taking ten bullets and O'Donnell two, while the lorry driver, Patrick Vincent, was shot five times before he'd even left the cab of his vehicle.

During the mêlée, a stray bullet ricocheted into the church's fuel-storage tank, igniting the oil and sending flames shooting up the side of the building. As the roof caught, the blaze lit up the sky, casting crazy shadows and adding to the confusion.

The fourth IRA man, Sean O'Farrell, reacted quickest to the ambush, turning and sprinting away through the churchyard. SAS troopers followed: he managed to cover 100 yards (91 m) before the conflagration on the church roof suddenly lit up his escape – he was shot five times while trying to scramble over a fence.

Also in the car park were the two waiting getaway drivers. Both took bullets, but after surrendering, were taken prisoner alive.

The attackers of Coalisland had their brief moment of victory – but they had also paid the ultimate price for it. Once again, the SAS had acted swiftly and mercilessly. Once again, the ambush had resulted in the deaths of all the IRA men directly involved in the attack. And once again, the manner of the ambush remained controversial: thirty years after the incident, in the summer of 2022, a court in Belfast ruled that an inquest into the deaths of the four IRA men would take place the following year.

The Clonoe ambush represents the effective end of 'shoot to kill' operations in Northern Ireland: afterwards, the SAS would not kill another IRA member in the province.

OPERATION TANGO

BOSNIA, 10 JULY 1997

THE SCENES INSIDE the prison camp at Omarska were a grim mirror of the horrors of Bergen-Belsen. The wasted and emaciated bodies, the skeletal and diseased men and women barely clinging on to life, the mass graves, the stench and rot and filth, the depravity and dehumanization of thousands ... the nightmare that had confronted Lieutenant Randall and Major Tonkin in the woods of northern Germany was made real again, in the 1990s, in Bosnia.

In 1992 the euphoria that followed the breakup of the former communist state of Yugoslavia had quickly soured and spilled into war. Catholic Croats, Orthodox Serbs and Bosnian Muslims who had previously been united under one flag were now fatally pitted against each other. Over just three years, some 100,000 people were killed, and a further 2 million displaced.

It was the war in Bosnia that gave rise to the term 'ethnic cleansing', as the ultra-nationalist Serb SDS party led by Radovan Karadžić embarked on a terror campaign aimed at ridding Bosnia of all non-Serbs.

Over 600 so-called 'detention centres' were installed across Bosnia to incarcerate Bosnian and Croat civilians. Among them was the camp at Omarska, near the town of Prijedor in north-west Bosnia. Hundreds died there, from torture, from beatings, from starvation and from disease, for no reason other than their ethnicity, their bodies piled in mass graves dug by their fellow prisoners.

The men who ordered and oversaw such atrocities had to be brought to account. One way or another.

◆ ◆ ◆

By 1997, the United Nations was ostensibly enforcing peace in Bosnia, but despite the reduction in outright fighting, two years after the ceasefire Serbian politicians and military leaders remained at large, apparently secure in the knowledge they were untouchable by the United Nations. For Prime Minister Tony Blair, who had recently won the British General Election with a huge majority, and US President Bill Clinton, secure in a second term in power, the situation was not only untenable, but unconscionable.

In top secret, plans were drawn up to finally arrest the war criminals.

The SAS had been active in Bosnia with the UN Peacekeeping Force since the United Nations had first become involved in the war, carrying out non-combat roles including surveillance and liaison work. Now it was given the task of finding and apprehending some of the conflict's most notorious figures.

It would not be a case of simply flashing a badge and a warrant. The targets were still influential and powerful men, capable of inflaming tensions in the region if given the chance, or provocation. The operation to detain them had to be laser-precise.

The SAS got to work.

It was decided that the first two targets would both be men

who had been instrumental in the horrors of the Omarska camp. If they could be taken without sparking a violent reaction from their support, more would follow.

Milan Kovačević was the former mayor of Prijedor; as the man in charge of the region in 1992, he had overseen the organized and systematic attempts to rid the municipality of all Bosnian Muslims and Croats. Kovačević gave the orders for Serbian forces to attack villages and kill civilians, as well as to round up survivors and intern them in the concentration camps.

Kovačević's right-hand man was Simo Drljača, the one-time Prijedor chief of police and a leading figure in the extreme SDS party. Kovačević gave the orders; Drljača carried them out – and did so with a ruthless and savage zeal, marching civilians at gunpoint from their homes to near-certain death at Omarska. When television reporters finally entered the camp in August 1992, exposing the scale of brutality and suffering inside, Drljača himself was there, smiling for the cameras. 'Why are they so thin?' he asked, mockingly. 'It's Ramadan! They're all fasting!'

Five years later, both had been indicted and charged by The Hague tribunal with war crimes including complicity to genocide; but both remained untouched by the law. Kovačević had taken up a position as director of Prijedor hospital, Drljača was enjoying a leisurely retirement, spending most of his time fishing.

They didn't know it, but time was running out for both men.

For weeks their every movement had been carefully tracked by undercover SAS operatives, the teams building up a meticulous record of each man's daily routine. Both were watched twenty-four hours a day: the routes they took to and from work, who they spoke to, what they spoke about, their hobbies and leisure activities, the bars and restaurants they frequented, the cars they drove, the coffee they drank ... every detail of their life was logged, documented, used to prepare and build a plan for their eventual apprehension. When the moment came, the SAS wanted nothing left to chance.

Finally, they were ready. The two teams that made up Operation Tango struck simultaneously, at 09.30 hours on 10 July 1997.

◆ ◆ ◆

In the reception area at Prijedor hospital, the man behind the desk barely looked twice at the Red Cross officials as they opened the main doors and approached his window. Since the end of the war, the Red Cross were a near-constant presence in the town, and naturally, much of their business was centred around the hospital.

The men nodded at him as they strolled confidently past. If the receptionist had taken a second glance, he might have reflected that they looked remarkably well-built compared to the usual charity workers he saw. Doctors weren't normally so muscular, their administrators even less so.

Once past reception the team moved fast through the hospital, making their way through corridors and up stairs on a route memorized and rehearsed to the point where each of them could have done it blindfolded.

Outside a door marked 'Director', they stopped. In absolute silence, each of them drew their 9-mm Browning pistols. They did not bother to knock.

If Milan Kovačević was surprised to see the SAS men burst into his office, he did a very good job of hiding it. With a sigh he raised both hands in the air. He knew the game was up. Fifteen minutes later he was handcuffed on a helicopter on the first leg of a journey to The Hague.

At exactly the same time as the SAS men were strolling through Prejidor hospital reception, another seven-man squad was moving against Simo Drljača, a few miles into the countryside outside Prijedor.

Their operation was a little less straightforward. Drljača was on an extended fishing trip with three friends, spending all day on the shores of the lake drinking and joking and occasionally even landing a fish. Entrenched in the undergrowth, the SAS men had watched the party for days, barely moving, noting that the former police chief still carried his pistol holstered at his hip. The previous weeks of surveillance had indicated that the other men should not be a threat, but nobody was going to take any chances.

At 09.30 the SAS men broke cover, rising out of the bushes by Drljača's camp, weapons drawn, safety catches off. One warning was shouted: 'We are here to arrest you.'

Drljača was not going to go as meekly as his former mayor had. His hands did not move up, but rather down and to his side – and his training meant he knew what he was doing. He managed to squeeze out a shot – wounding one of the troopers in the leg – before crumpling under a hail of fire himself. Even as he fell, the commandos moved in on his companions: they surrendered without resistance and were later released without arrest.

Simo Drljača was dead; Milan Kovačević was incarcerated – and would die of a heart attack while still in custody a year later. The first arrests of Bosnia's indicted war criminals had been a success – and thanks to the SAS, at long last, the United Nations was asserting its authority in the region. A message had been sent to all those responsible for the appalling crimes committed during the Bosnian War: you are no longer safe. We are coming for you.

OPERATION ENSUE

SERBIA, 27 SEPTEMBER 1998

STRICTLY SPEAKING, the SAS squad entrenched deep in the forest near Zlatibor in western Serbia were not behind enemy lines, but every man among them knew that for all intents and purposes, the phrase was a matter of semantics. The bottom line was, if their position was compromised, their lives would be in grave danger.

Serbia was no longer at war with Bosnia – but the state was very much still a law unto itself. A non-Serbian military unit on active duty in the country would be seen as a threat, and if that unit happened to be a British special forces patrol tasked with the kidnap of a former Serbian commander and, to some at least, hero of the Bosnian War, yet more so.

Even if they did have authorization from the United Nations. Especially if they had authorization from the United Nations.

The forest hummed and buzzed, midges and insects swarming around the troopers as they inched forward from positions they had held for days, watching, waiting, circling the log cabin, monitoring not only the activity inside but also all possible routes to and from the remote building. A single dirt track was easily monitored, but in these dense woods a small army with the skill and wherewithal could approach from any direction almost completely undetected. The SAS team knew that, because that's exactly what they had done.

A silent signal given and received, and it was on. Acting as one man, the unit moved on log cabin. With a single blow the door was obliterated and they were in.

The lone figure inside was taken completely by surprise. Relaxing in an easy chair by an open fire, he barely had time to move before the SAS men were on top of him. A gag placed around his mouth stifled a scream, another wrapped around his eyes blinded him before he could see enough of his assailants to later recognize them. Rough hands wrenched his arms behind his back, cable ties lashing his wrists together; other hands wrestled him upright and propelled him towards the door.

Blind, mute, bound and terrified, he was out of the cabin and bundled into the back of a four-by-four. Not a word was spoken as the vehicle sped along the pitch-black forest path, headlights off, heading north towards the border, and Bosnia.

◆ ◆ ◆

Stevan Todorović was thirty-five years old when the war broke out, and had been appointed chief of police for the Bosanski Šamac region of northern Bosnia. He oversaw what the United Nations later described as a brutal 'campaign of terror' against the Croat and Muslim population, responsible for beatings, torture, rapes and murders as part of the Serbian ethnic cleansing policy in the region. His indictment stated that 'in 1991, almost 17,000 Bosnian Croats and Muslims, of a total population of about 33,000, lived in the municipality of Bosanski Šamac. By May 1995, fewer than 300 of the Bosnian Croat and Muslim residents remained.'

The charges against Todorović included five counts of Grave Breaches of the Geneva Conventions (including wilful killing, inhumane treatment and torture) and five counts of Crimes Against Humanity, including murder and rape. Witnesses described how on one occasion he had personally beaten a man to death in the hallway of the Bosanski Šamac police station, and on another forced six men to perform sexual acts on each other in the station, before beating them too.

Unlike other war criminals such as Simo Drljača and Milan Kovačević, after his indictment he had fled to Serbia, where, under the protection of President Milošević – who would later be charged with sixty-six counts of Crimes Against Humanity himself – he believed himself beyond the reach of the UN.

The SAS had other ideas. After tracking his location to a remote cabin in the forest around 50 miles (80 km) over the Serbian border, they set about bringing Todorović to justice. On the night of 27 September 1998, they sprung the trap.

◆ ◆ ◆

Kidnapping Todorović was one thing. Getting him out of Serbia was another altogether. As the four-by-four containing the seven commandos and their struggling captive raced through the woods in absolute darkness, the driver not daring to put the lights on and trusting to a little luck and a lot of skill not to crash into anything, the SAS men knew that, far from the operation being nearly over, the most dangerous part was only just beginning.

If they were to be challenged by Serbian forces, shooting would surely follow. And once the shooting began, it would be a case of kill or be killed. Arresting an indicted war criminal – even in Serbia – was politically and legally justifiable, but British forces engaged in open combat against the Serbian military would be a trickier prospect for the government and the UN to account for. The SAS not only had to get Todorović safely over the border; they had to do so without anyone seeing or hearing anything about it.

After an hour's tense, bumpy drive, they skidded to a stop in a small clearing on the banks of the Drina river, which forms the border between Serbia and Bosnia. In absolute silence, they jumped from the vehicle and set about inflating two five-man Zodiac rubber boats. Even in the dark, the process took just minutes. The prisoner was bundled into one dinghy along with four of the commandos, while the other three men launched the second boat.

The four-by-four was left on the bank, and both Zodiacs slipped through the water, troopers training guns fore and aft against any last-minute attacks. The current was strong and treacherous, the water black and freezing, but the SAS men were stronger. In preparation for this operation they had practised the crossing dozens of times and in all conditions; within minutes they were on the far bank, and hauling the boats to shore.

The final leg of Stevan Todorović's nightmarish journey was a helicopter ride to the US base at Tuzla in Bosnia, another 100 miles (161 km) north, where he would later be transferred to the War Crimes Commission at The Hague. It was only after he landed at Tuzla that his gag and blindfold were removed.

As light flooded his eyes and he blinked and gasped, the first face the former police chief was confronted with belonged to a grinning US officer. 'So you thought you were safe over there, did you?' the American asked.

◆ ◆ ◆

Stevan Todorović stood trial for his crimes before the UN International Criminal Tribunal for the Former Yugoslavia, and pleaded not guilty.

In his defence he claimed 'a great deal of fear, panic, fatigue, stress, and at times alcohol, too, influenced my actions', and that 'I lacked courage to prevent the illegal and inhuman activities that were going on.'

The court disagreed. In 2001 a guilty verdict was returned and he was sentenced to ten years in prison.

The SAS extraction of Todorović from inside Serbia marked another step forward in the mission to bring all the perpetrators of war crimes in the former Yugoslavia to account for their actions. So much so that, rather than keep the details of how he was captured classified, as would be usual in such a sensitive special forces operation, the British openly let it be known that the SAS had carried out the raid, with one senior official reportedly saying: 'It's a deliberate frightener for Milošević. That's policy now.'

The message was clear. There would be nowhere to hide, not even in Serbia.

In 2017 the International Criminal Tribunal for the Former Yugoslavia was finally wound down. Since 1993 it had successfully indicted 161 individuals on war crimes and genocide charges, with ninety of those convicted and sentenced. Just twenty-one of the accused were acquitted at trial – and three of those acquittals were later overturned on appeal.

Among those to face justice was Serbian President Slobodan Milošević, the first sitting head of state to ever be indicted for war crimes. He was found dead in his prison cell at The Hague in March 2006, midway through his trial.

Stevan Todorović was released from prison in 2005, on credit for time served since his arrest in 1998. A year later his body was found at his home. He had died from a single gunshot to the head; his hand still gripped a pistol.

OPERATION BARRAS

SIERRA LEONE, 10 SEPTEMBER 2000

FIRST LIGHT BROKE at 06.16 hours, a pale September dawn bleeding the skies above the Sierra Leone jungle – and with it came the whirr of helicopter blades. Two Lynx attack machines and three powerful Chinook troop carriers flew low and fast along the Rokel Creek from their base in Hastings, near the capital Freetown, speeding towards a firefight on which the whole of Britain's armed presence in west Africa depended.

The mission: to extract five soldiers of the Royal Irish Regiment and their Sierra Leone Army liaison officer, all held hostage for over two weeks by a well-armed, highly aggressive and dangerously unpredictable rebel militia group known as the West Side Boys.

At stake was not just the lives of the six hostages, and of the men leading the raid to free them, but the entire fragile humanitarian operation in Sierra Leone itself. With the West Side Boys growing in power and confidence, failure would mean not only humiliation for the British military, but disaster for a country that had been torn apart by nine years of bloody and brutal civil war.

It took a little under fifteen minutes for the helicopters to reach their target – the West Side Boys' bases in the abandoned villages of Gberi Bana and Magbeni, on opposite sides of Rokel Creek. As they flew in, a covert SAS observation team emplaced by the villages sprang a surprise attack from the jungle, and a fierce battle began.

◆ ◆ ◆

Operation Barras had been weeks in the planning and was conducted on a strict need-to-know basis: even the negotiating team who had been in talks with the West Side Boys since the capture of the hostages were not told when or how the operation was going to take place. Success depended on this secrecy – and on the speed, precision and deadly efficiency with which the special forces executed their mission. It could so easily have gone horribly wrong.

Seventeen days earlier, on 25 August 2000, Major Alan Marshall of the Royal Irish Regiment had made a disastrous decision. After hearing reports that the rebels had begun to disarm, he took his patrol of eleven men, as well as Lieutenant Musa Bangura of the Sierra Leone Army, off the main road near the town of Masiaka, in the jungles in the west of Sierra Leone, and onto the dirt track towards Magbeni to investigate.

Marshall was leading his men into a trap.

Magbeni was one of hundreds of rural villages gutted by the civil war that had by that time accounted for some 70,000 casualties and over 2.5 million displaced people. The village was situated deep in the jungle some 43 miles (70 km) from the capital Freetown. Its inhabitants had once eked out a living mining sand for construction, but by 2000 most had either fled or been killed and – along with nearby Gberi Bana – the ragtag collection of huts that remained served as the main base for the West Side Boys militia gang. What locals remained were kept in appalling conditions, with the women especially suffering horrific abuse as sex slaves.

Dense jungle surrounded the village, the only entrance being a single dirt track, at the end of which was a clearing. The perfect conditions, in other words, for an ambush.

And so the trap was sprung. As the patrol drove into the clearing, a Bedford truck on which an anti-aircraft gun had been mounted swung in to cut off their escape, and a large, heavily armed group of the rebel militia emerged from the village and surrounded them. Forced at gunpoint from their Land Rovers, the British troops were beaten, tied up, and taken in canoes across the creek to Gberi Bana, an even more inaccessible village, all but swallowed up by the jungle altogether.

Corporal Ian Getty was among the captured soldiers. 'There was like a clearing, you couldn't see the road 'cos of the jungle either side of it,' he said in a 2007 interview archived by the National Army Museum. 'So we basically just drove into this clearing and there was about 150 of them. But they had a van with, what do you call them, the big Russian guns. And they brought it in behind us and they faced up so we couldn't back out, and then kicked the shit out of us, and took our guns.'

Marshall's men had been in Sierra Leone with Britain's humanitarian and peacekeeping force. After first arriving in May as part of a non-combatant operation to evacuate foreign nationals from the country, British troops had stayed on to train Sierra Leone's army and support the United Nations Mission as it struggled to establish some sort of stability after the chaos of the civil war.

By far the nastiest combatants in that war had been the West

Side Boys. The militia group had originally formed in 1998 as a wing of the rebel army fighting the government, before switching sides ... and then switching back again. By August 2000 they were a law unto themselves, a volatile, unpredictable bandit outfit numbering hundreds strong, fuelled by alcohol, drugs and violence.

Negotiating with them would not be easy. Put in charge of trying to secure the hostages' release was Lieutenant Colonel Simon Fordham, commander of 1st Battalion Irish Regiment. His first priority was to deal with the leader of the gang, a skinny twenty-five-year-old man dressed in army fatigues and flip-flops called Foday Kallay. Among Kallay's quirks were an obsession with American gangster rap and an insistence on being referred to as 'Brigadier', but if Kallay seemed slightly ridiculous, he was also a cold-blooded killer, with a particular fondness for either recruiting the children of his victims into his army, or mutilating them so they could not later fight against him.

Speaking in 2009, in another interview now archived by the National Army Museum, Lieutenant Colonel Fordham described the tensions at their first meeting.

'It was pretty volatile,' he remembered. 'It was quite clear something had gone on because these rebels were in a highly agitated state. Very nervous. Very trigger-happy. Lots of weapons around. I could sense that this was a situation that we had to treat carefully because there was a very strong sense of ... a small mistake here could mean that we could get into a shooting match quite quickly. We were in a situation that was very dangerous, had the potential to become very violent, and people's lives were at stake.'

Lieutenant Colonel Fordham demanded proof that the hostages were still alive, and on 29 August, Kallay brought along two men – Major Alan Marshall, and Captain Ed Flaherty. And that's when something extraordinary happened.

'As [Flaherty] came forward he saluted, shook hands with me, and as we shook hands I realised there was something in the hand and it was a pen top,' Fordham said.

Flaherty secretly palmed the pen top to the lieutenant colonel as they shook hands, and the latter pocketed it without any of the guards noticing. Inside was a tiny roll of paper, on which had been drawn a map of the village.

'And later, as we looked at it, it was a sketched diagram that had been drawn of where they were kept,' Fordham said. 'The layout of the village, where the sentries were, what the routine was, and all the rest of it.'

Captain Flaherty's bravery in passing along his crude map would be a crucial factor in the later planning of the operation.

As negotiations continued, however, Kallay's demands became ever-more unrealistic. Five hostages were released in exchange for a satellite phone on 31 August, but following that success, talks broke down. Kallay demanded a renegotiation of the fragile peace accord that had ended the civil war, the release of prisoners held by the Sierra Leone authorities, immunity from prosecution, acceptance to the re-formed Sierra Leone Army, and finally, most bizarrely, safe passage to the UK and a university education for his men.

Things were further hampered by the volatility of the West Side Boys themselves. The threat of sudden violence was ever present, and Kallay – frequently drunk and under the influence of drugs – would often forget what had been discussed or agreed the previous day.

While Lieutenant Colonel Fordham struggled, behind the scenes another plan was being put together. Two SAS men had joined the negotiating team, posing as Royal Irish officers in order to gather intelligence on the strength of the West Side Boys' weaponry and defences. Meanwhile, two further SAS reconnaissance teams had covertly made their way up Rokel Creek to hide in the jungle near Gberi Bana and Magbeni. They would remain in deep cover for three days in gruelling 'hard routine' conditions, enduring the harsh heat and fetid rain of the Sierra Leone jungle, bitten by insects and mosquitos, and under the constant threat of discovery by militia patrols. Their task: to monitor the rebels' movements and gather intelligence on weapon placements and viable helicopter landing sites.

As the relationship between Lieutenant Colonel Fordham and Foday Kallay disintegrated, the urgency increased. The deep-cover teams reported that Kallay was planning to move the hostages further into the jungle, or possibly execute them outright. The final straw came on 9 September, when a West Side Boys spokesman calling himself 'Colonel Cambodia' stated that the remaining six prisoners would only be released after a new Sierra Leone government was formed.

At an emergency COBRA meeting in London, the order was given to launch Operation Barras at first light the following day.

◆ ◆ ◆

The helicopters that took off from Freetown on 10 September held not only SAS troops from 'D' Squadron, 22 SAS, but also a support group drawn from 1st Battalion Paras. The plan – like all good plans – was simple. It was also – as SAS operations all too often are – incredibly high-risk.

There were to be two simultaneous assaults: the SAS would attack the main West Side Boys force in Gberi Bana with the aim of extracting the hostages as quickly as possible, while at the same time the Paras would target Magbeni on the other side of the creek, cutting off the militia's reinforcements and preventing them from intervening in the rescue mission. Both assaults would be supported by the emplaced SAS teams hiding in the jungle.

As the helicopters raced up Rokel Creek that morning, the sound of their blades tore through the early-morning air. This was the moment of greatest peril: Kallay's militia might have been an erratic, unpredictable gang of thugs, bandits and murderers, but they were also ferocious fighters – and extremely well-armed. They would not hesitate to execute the prisoners if the rescue team did not get there in time.

The choppers came in fast and under intense fire. The two Lynx attack helicopters strafed the villages, targeting the heavy weapons already identified by the recon teams, while the three Chinooks flew so low that the downdraft tore off the corrugated roofs of the huts in Gberi Bana.

As the West Side Boys scrambled to repel the raid, the observation teams ambushed the villages from their hidden positions. Their aim was to keep the rebels busy enough to prevent any attempt to kill the hostages before the Chinooks could unload.

SAS troops fast-roped into the village – sliding down the rope at speed and with no safety harness, trusting in their gloves to prevent friction burns. Almost immediately they sustained their first serious casualty, when Trooper Bradley Tinnion was shot in the flank. He was dragged back to the helicopter but later died from the wound, despite intensive resuscitation attempts. It was Tinnion's first operational deployment as an SAS trooper.

And still the fighting intensified. Spreading into teams, 'D' Squadron fought hut-to-hut, returning whatever the West Side Boys threw at them with interest, clearing the village, driving the resistance back into the jungle and killing at least twenty-five gang members, while another team used Flaherty's scribbled map to locate and rescue the hostages.

In his 2007 National Army Museum interview, Corporal Ian Getty described the scenes from inside the hut where they had been held.

'That was one of their things: no helicopters over the top of them,' he said. 'So there'd been no helicopters for seventeen days basically since it happened. But that day we heard the helicopter in the morning and it woke everyone up, so it was quite close. And we could hear the West Side Boys starting to get up and hear it. And it turned around and we could hear it going away and so obviously we were quite relieved because they said they were going to shoot us if a helicopter comes over.

'Then we heard it turning back and this time it just did the full run-in and just opened up with the guns. And then, it must have been about ten seconds later, they were kicking the door in. The guy just says, "Stay there. Stay down." Then you heard them say there was some fighting outside.

'We stayed in that room. Then … they [the SAS] came and got us all in a line, ran up to another house where they had like a big football pitch where they were landing the helicopters, into the helicopter and away.

'All the fighting was being done in the jungle round the sides. Anyone in the village was dead.'

◆ ◆ ◆

It took only twenty minutes from the first Lynx attack to airlift all six hostages to safety. Meanwhile, as the Paras simultaneously attacked Magbeni in an equally successful assault, rescuing twenty-one civilians who had been kept as slaves, the West Side Boys finally gave up. At least two dozen of them were dead (some reports estimate up to eighty fatalities) and a further eighteen, including leader Foday Kallay, were taken prisoner. The rest had fled.

On the British side there had been the loss of Trooper Tinnion, and a further twelve men wounded, but these casualties notwithstanding, the operation was considered one of the SAS's most stunning victories.

Carried out in extraordinarily difficult conditions and with a minimum of intelligence, the assault had not only successfully rescued twenty-seven hostages for the loss of just one British life, but also ended the West Side Boys' reign of terror for good. In the weeks that followed the raid, some 370 of them surrendered to the United Nations Mission in Sierra Leone.

All the British troops – SAS and Paras alike – who saw service in Operation Barras received the Operational Service Medal for Sierra Leone. In addition, gallantry medals, including two Conspicuous Gallantry Crosses, Britain's second-highest award after the Victoria Cross for bravery in combat, were also awarded. Trooper Tinnion received a posthumous Mention in Despatches.

Operation Barras was the first time since its inception in 1941 that the SAS had been deployed to rescue other members of the

British army, and the success of the cooperation between the SAS and the Paras led to the creation of the Special Forces Support Group – a unique unit whose role is to act as a force multiplier for the SAS on complex operations and that has since become integral to operations in Afghanistan and Iraq.

In his National Army Museum interview, Lieutenant Colonel Simon Fordham reflected upon the greater impact Operation Barras was to have for UK Special Forces.

'The operation was a tremendous success because it was carried out by people that were highly skilled and had the motivation of rescuing fellow soldiers,' he said. 'It was a difficult and daring operation that went particularly well. And I think it's fair to say that, with subsequent operations in Iraq and ... Afghanistan, this was the first kind of dirty and dangerous operation that reminded ... people that while we had been involved in quite a lot of counter-revolutionary and counter-terrorist operations, we hadn't had this kind of close-quarter fighting with the enemy for a long time.'

It would not be long before the SAS were once again engaged in this new kind of 'dirty and dangerous' operation. Almost exactly one year later, the world would change forever.

PART 3

POST
9/11

CAPTURE OF H2 AND H3 AIRBASES

IRAQ, 21 MARCH 2003

THE SO-CALLED 'FIRST GULF WAR' that followed Iraq's invasion of Kuwait had done nothing to ease tensions in the Middle East – if anything, the failure by the US- and British-led coalition to effect regime change within Iraq itself only emboldened that country's president, Saddam Hussein. The way he span it, the West stopped short of invading Iraq because they were incapable of doing so, or afraid of doing so, or both. In the decade that followed, despite the establishment of a no-fly zone, economic sanctions, and regular inspections by the United Nations to ensure the country was not developing weapons of mass destruction, Iraq, and Saddam Hussein, only grew more belligerent.

For many, especially in America, the job felt half-done.

And then something happened that nobody could have predicted.

On the morning of 11 September 2001, nineteen militant Islamist terrorists hijacked four passenger jets travelling to California. Two of the planes were crashed into the twin towers of the World Trade Center in New York. A third flew into the Pentagon in Virginia, and the fourth was downed by its passengers in a field in Pennsylvania before it could reach its target of Washington DC.

Nearly 3,000 died, in what was the deadliest terrorist attack on

American soil in US history.

The Islamist terror group al-Qaeda claimed responsibility for 9/11 and a little over a month later, the US launched an invasion of Afghanistan in an attempt to capture its leader, Osama bin Laden. At the same time, and in secret, plans began to be drawn up to finally get rid of Saddam Hussein.

Although a direct link between Iraq and the 11 September attacks has since been definitively discredited, Saddam Hussein's regime had nonetheless been pushing its luck for years. As early as 1998, the Iraqi government had suspended cooperation with United Nations weapons inspectors sent to monitor its dismantling of chemical, biological and nuclear weapons development facilities; after the al-Qaeda attacks, whispers began to circulate not only that Iraq still had these weapons of mass destruction, but that they posed a direct threat to the populations of both America and the UK.

In January 2002, President George Bush declared: 'The United States of America will not permit the world's most dangerous regimes to threaten us with the world's most destructive weapons.'

A little over a year later, just before dawn on 20 March 2003, a coalition of thirty-nine governments led by the US, the British and the Australians, invaded Iraq.

The SAS were at war once more.

◆ ◆ ◆

One hundred and sixty thousand troops, along with massive air support, were tasked with toppling Saddam Hussein's regime. Around 45,000 of these were British – and some 2,000 were special forces.

One of the first ground actions of the war was to fall to the SAS in a joint operation between the British and Australian wings of the force. The main thrust of the coalition armies was invading from the south-east, but a significant pincer movement would be moving towards Baghdad from Jordan, to the west of Iraq – and vital to their plans was securing forward operating bases along the Baghdad Highway, a 320-mile (515-km) road cutting straight through the desert from the Jordanian border to Iraq's capital.

The highway was crucial – not only as the main artery to Baghdad, but also as the principal exit route for the thousands of refugees expected to flood west to Jordan. Securing it was a military priority, and a humanitarian necessity.

The road would not be lightly defended, and two of the biggest obstacles to any progress along it were the twin airbases known as H2 and H3. From these positions, the Iraqi army could launch attacks against coalition aircraft and armour, as well as operate deadly Scud missile launchers capable of striking at targets hundreds of miles away in Jordan and even Israel.

Both bases were expected to be heavily fortified, and the SAS knew from the experiences of the men from Bravo Two Zero patrol a decade earlier just how vicious the Iraqi military could be. The world expected an easy win, but on the desert floor, where it mattered, nothing was being taken for granted.

The airstrips were two stark clusters of concrete bunkers lying squat and solid in the windswept plains: H3 was just 45 miles (72 km) from the border, H2 another 65 miles (105 km) along the highway to Baghdad. The success of the operation rested on capturing them both more or less simultaneously: take only one and it would be wide open to bombardment from the other, not to mention the risk a fully armed and operational Iraqi fortress would pose to the main body of the invading coalition army, or to refugees fleeing along the highway to Jordan.

On 21 January, as the coalition began its aerial bombardment of Iraq, 200 SAS troopers from 'B' and 'D' squadrons as well as Australian 1 Squadron SAS were flown by RAF Chinook helicopters across the border. One force was dropped close to H3 airbase, the other sped further east, towards H2. Both were equipped with specially adapted Land Rovers armed with heavy machine guns.

As it turned out, taking H2 was easier than anticipated.

After the drop the plan was to encircle the base and then, once the surrounding area was secured, radio in a series of air strikes against the defenders inside. After the RAF had done their thing, the SAS would move in.

The H2 team watched as the bombers screamed over, their payload transforming the desert into a blinding wall of sand and fire and shrapnel. After the dust cleared, they launched their own assault. Flanking teams covered the outlying buildings, spraying them with fire as the main force sped in the Land Rovers towards the central body of the base, splitting up to secure watchtowers, control buildings and central offices.

Resistance was minimal; all the buildings were taken without serious opposition. H2 was either considered less strategically important than the coalition had anticipated, or else it was a decoy. Either way, the SAS had control of the base.

Sixty-five miles (105 km) west, things were not so straightforward.

Like their colleagues at H2, the squad had moved quickly to

establish a secure position from which to call in air strikes against the base. Unlike their colleagues at H2, they found themselves facing a fully manned and heavily armed opposition. A full battalion of the Iraqi army, backed up by significant heavy artillery, defended H3, and they were determined to repel any assault.

Static and mobile anti-aircraft weaponry were directed not only at the incoming coalition planes, but at the SAS troops themselves. Even with their armoured Land Rovers, the British and Australians were seriously outmanned, and seriously outgunned.

Attack was not an option – but not for long.

Reinforcements joined them: Royal Marines from 45 Commando, as well as specialist US Delta Force and Green Beret troops. The defenders were now effectively trapped in their own base – and once again, the RAF were called in. For twenty-four straight hours H3 was pummelled by precision air strikes, targeting the heavy guns and missile launchers, as well as the buildings in which the Iraqi troops cowered.

Before they had time to recover, they were hit on the ground too. In a concentrated assault, the SAS – their numbers bolstered by the marines and American special forces – swept in from all directions in a fast, devastating attack, Land Rover guns blazing.

The Iraqis never stood a chance. Within twenty minutes it was all over, many of H3's defenders fleeing into the desert, rather than face the wrath of the special forces men.

They left behind a huge cache of ammunition, as well as eighty anti-aircraft cannons and other heavy artillery. Had the Iraqi troops held out longer – or had the combination of air strikes and such a fierce ground assault by the SAS not inflicted such damage on their morale – H3 could have been a serious threat to any progress along the Baghdad Highway.

◆ ◆ ◆

Both airbases were now secured, and the coalition forces had forward operating bases in Iraq from which to advance on Baghdad. Next the SAS turned their attention to the wide expanse of the Iraq wilderness, and the threat of mobile Scud missile launchers.

H2 and H3 were handed over to the Royal Marines and US Army Rangers and the British special forces embarked on a deadly cat-and-mouse game played out across thousands of square miles of desert.

Unmanned drones and spotter planes patrolled the skies night and day, scanning the ground for signs of Iraqi patrols or Scud units; as soon as they registered enemy movement, the SAS were despatched.

The Land Rovers meant the commandos could strike fast and hard, speeding into firefights that would often be as brief as they were decisive. Appearing from nowhere, and with an apparent sixth sense for where their targets would be, the SAS harried and hounded the Iraqi army, taking control of the desert, nullifying the threat of the Scud missiles.

According to one military source quoted in *Jane's Defence Weekly* on 3 April 2003, Iraq's western desert had become a 'special forces playground'.

CAPTURE OF WATBAN AL-TIKRITI

IRAQ, 13 APRIL 2003

THE SIX-MAN SAS squad observed their target carefully. They had been watching him for days, ever since intelligence had first reported him fleeing the city of Tikrit as the Americans stormed Baghdad, hoisting US flags and tearing down statues. For 230 miles (370 km) they had tracked him, deep undercover, looking without being seen, monitoring his every movement as he made his careful way north and west, heading towards what looked very much like a bid for the Syrian border.

Up to this point, they had been content only to watch. The target, despite the fall of Baghdad and the collapse of the Iraqi regime, remained a dangerous and influential man. He was rarely alone, often surrounded by what looked like bodyguards, and – in a counter-intuitive move that the SAS men would have respected as much as been frustrated by – had mostly avoided isolated and out-of-the-way places on his journey, despite his fugitive status.

Approaching and attempting to apprehend him in such circumstances could prove disastrous. With tensions in Iraq sky high, it was simply too great a risk to take. The whole of the Middle East was a tinderbox. They did not want to provide the spark that set it all off again.

But now, finally, at a checkpoint near the town of Rabia, 60 miles (97 km) north-west of Mosul and hard against the Syrian border, they had their chance.

For the umpteenth time, they checked the packs of specially commissioned playing cards each man had been issued with. Five of spades. Watban Ibrahim Hasan al-Tikriti. Half-brother of Saddam Hussein himself.

◆ ◆ ◆

To the outside world at least, the Iraq War ended on 9 April 2003, when after just a few weeks of fighting, coalition forces took the Iraqi capital Baghdad, ending Saddam Hussein's twenty-four-year rule and effectively killing off any hope of a military counter-offensive.

But it was not, despite President Bush's subsequent 'Mission accomplished' speech, anything like the end of the war. Baghdad may have fallen and Saddam Hussein no longer been president, but there was still plenty of work to be done. The mission was far from accomplished.

Saddam Hussein had escaped capture, fleeing Baghdad along with many of his top officials – and as long as they were out there somewhere, at large and with their whereabouts unknown, they remained a threat.

The territory was won, but the people of Iraq were not. The US- and British-led invasion had fostered huge anti-Western resentment in the region, something fundamentalist and extremist Islamic groups were quick to exploit. Ironically, al-Qaeda was now a serious presence in Iraq, and they, along with other militant terrorist factions, continued the fight the Iraqi army could not win, taking the conflict underground with small – but deadly – terror attacks on the British and American bases.

Suicide bombers were commonplace, improvised explosive devices an everyday danger. Even as the coalition began a 'hearts-and-minds' campaign to win the affection – or if not affection at least not outright enmity – of the Iraqi people, they were forced to remain in a state of near-total vigilance against the threat of bombings, ambushes and other attacks.

Under such precarious circumstances, it was vital that the coalition military commanders neutralized those disappeared former Iraqi leaders who might provide a banner for the insurgents to rally around. Politicians, generals and other key figures in Saddam Hussein's regime – as well as the former president himself – had to be found, and brought to justice.

Uniquely adapted decks of cards had been issued to every soldier on the ground in Iraq, the traditional markings replaced by images of the fifty-two most wanted men of the former regime. Each card showed an image of the fugitive, along with his name, rank or job title, and (former) address. The most valuable card in the pack, the ace of spades, was Saddam himself, his sons Qusay and Uday assigned the aces of clubs and hearts respectively.

Every coalition soldier in Iraq may have had a deck of these cards, but only a few men were tasked with actively seeking out the targets. And if finding them was to prove difficult enough, bringing them safely to justice would be far trickier still.

A natural fit for the SAS, in other words.

Along with the elite US special forces outfit Delta Force, the SAS took the lead in clearing the coalition's deck of cards. In the days, weeks and months that followed the routing of Baghdad, they became bounty hunters.

These missions were classified at the very highest level, often so secret that they weren't officially happening at all. Even today, details remain closely guarded, the identities of the men involved hidden, and many of the means and methods of the SAS's actions kept from public knowledge.

◆ ◆ ◆

There was a good reason Watban Ibrahim Hasan al-Tikriti had been included in the 'Wanted: dead or alive' deck.

The fifty-one-year-old was Iraq's former Interior Minister and a half-brother of Saddam Hussein on his mother's side. He was also, like so many senior figures in that regime, a vicious and sadistic monster.

A close advisor of Saddam's from his rise to power in 1979, he was a key figure in the genocidal campaign against the Kurdish people of northern Iraq in 1988, when as many as 100,000 were killed, and the male Kurdish population of northern Iraq all but wiped out.

As Interior Minister he was accused of overseeing the torture and execution of hundreds of prisoners – even, it was alleged, personally attending and sometimes videotaping the executions to enjoy replaying them at his leisure – as well as authorizing the mass killings of Shi'ite Muslims after the first Gulf War.

His rising profile and increasing power had similarly made him a subject of the intrigues, jealousies and backstabbings that also defined the highest levels of Saddam's brutal regime: in 1995, an argument with Saddam's son Uday escalated into violence – and ended with Uday shooting him nine times in the leg. Permanently crippled, Watban was reposted to the city of Tikrit, 90 miles (145 km) north of Baghdad, partly for his own safety, partly to deter any thoughts of revenge he might harbour.

The rivalry with Uday Hussein was irrelevant now. As the old regime fell, Watban knew the crimes he oversaw as Interior Minister made him a marked man. In a final desperate bid to evade justice, he was heading for Syria, and, so he hoped, obscurity and immunity.

The SAS had different ideas.

Watban had been travelling with bodyguards and under a false identity, but, despite the disguise, the man they had been tailing was undeniably him. From Tikrit to Mosul and beyond, he had thus far been able to travel unchallenged and with relative impunity, but to get any closer to Syria he would now have to pass through the final coalition checkpoint at Rabia, the last Iraqi town before the border. This was their chance.

The usual soldiers manning the checkpoint had been briefed as much as the need-to-know status of the operation allowed, and had moved aside to be replaced by the SAS squad. As Watban approached, forged documents in hand, they gave the outward impression of bored troopers tired of processing the endless stream of refugees from Iraq to Syria, but inwardly they remained hair-trigger alert. If Watban, or his men, were to put up a fight, the SAS needed that fight to be short, decisive and to cause a minimum of disruption that might alert any other hostile elements nearby.

As it turned out, the former Interior Minister had no more fight left in him. Watban surrendered meekly, the commandos quickly arresting him and whisking him away to an undisclosed base, where he was handed over to the US authorities.

The five of spades had been removed from the pack. Meticulous patience and careful planning had proved more effective than brute force. Sometimes the SAS did not need to go in all guns blazing.

◆ ◆ ◆

On 11 March 2009, along with his brother Sabawi – himself the former Director of the Iraq Intelligence Service and the six of diamonds in the 'most wanted' deck – Watban Ibrahim Hasan al-Tikriti was sentenced to death by hanging for his role in the execution of forty-two men in 1992, following the first Gulf War.

Neither of the brothers saw their sentences carried out. Although the US army handed Watban over to the Iraqi authorities in 2011, he remained imprisoned, finally dying from natural causes in August 2015. Sabawi had died of cancer in jail two years earlier.

At the time of writing, of the fifty-two members of Saddam Hussein's government pictured on the 'most wanted' playing cards, only four remain at large.

Uday and Qusay Hussein were killed in Mosul three months after Watban's capture, after a US-led operation to arrest them spiralled into a four-hour gun battle that also resulted in the death of Qusay's fourteen-year-old son Mustafa, and the wounding of four American special forces soldiers.

Five months after that, in December 2003, Saddam Hussein himself was discovered hiding in a foxhole near Tikrit by Delta Force soldiers. The former dictator was dishevelled and starving and surrendered without a fight; he was executed by the Iraqi government on 30 December 2006.

OPERATION ABALONE

IRAQ, 31 OCTOBER 2003

THE TWO TROOPERS from 'A' Squadron SAS inched towards the compound, senses straining, hearts hammering. The wreckage of high gates marked the house's perimeter; beyond them lay an open yard and a cluster of buildings, dirty white concrete walls pockmarked with fire and shrapnel, windows like the black sockets of a skull.

Minutes earlier, twelve men from the squadron had burst into this yard to secure one of those buildings in a manoeuvre practised hundreds of times before, but had run straight into a trap.

As they crashed through the gates, the blank windows of the house had suddenly come alive in a storm of lead and destruction, as jihadi insurgents inside opened up with everything they had. Russian-made AK-47s spewed bullets at the SAS men, deadly trajectories following them as they dived for cover – before the automatic gunfire was drowned out by the dreadful scream and blast of an RPG 7 anti-tank rocket.

The commandos had scattered, retreating back beyond the gates as fast as they dared through the hail of bullets, sustaining casualties as they ran.

Safely under cover once more, the commanding officer had run a quick headcount. Of the twelve who had stormed the gate, only ten had returned. Not knowing if the missing men were dead or only injured, he sent another two troopers back into the ambush zone to find out.

As they crept forward, the night air was still again, the swirls and clouds of dust, sand and dirt kicked up by the firefight beginning to lift a little. At the far end of the yard, the buildings were quiet, the windows once more black and inscrutable.

Warily, they moved onwards ... and suddenly they saw them. One man face down in the sand, motionless. As they watched, they could see blood pooling in a slow, dark, growing puddle around his head. The other man was on the far side of the yard, almost directly beneath the windows from which the gunfire and rockets had come. Also flat on his belly, he was bleeding, but alive and still holding his gun. He had laid his grenades on the ground beside him. Was this in readiness for a last-ditch defence? Or was he planning to launch a surprise kamikaze assault of his own?

Either way, his chances of survival would be next to zero. The two SAS men had to make a decision, and they had to make it now.

◆ ◆ ◆

Rounding up the most wanted men from Saddam Hussein's reign was a tactic that many political and military analysts feared would prove to be a double-edged sword. Resentment against Iraq's Western invaders had grown into a full-blown insurgency, and as new militant Islamist groups infiltrated the region, the danger was that another leader could emerge to fill the vacuum left by the removal of Saddam Hussein.

By the autumn of 2003, forty of the fifty-two men pictured on the playing cards hit list were either dead or imprisoned, but the country was, if anything, more unstable than it had been at the time of the invasion just six months before.

As it turned out, the risk was never of the militants coalescing around a leader from the former regime; rather, by removing whatever semblance of stability Iraq may have had under Saddam Hussein's rule, a Pandora's box had been opened ... and chaos inevitably followed.

From his hiding place in Afghanistan, 9/11 mastermind Osama bin Laden had called for a jihad, or holy war, in Iraq, and on the ground, al-Qaeda was growing in power and ambition across the entire Middle East. Worst of all, a new fundamentalist terror group calling themselves Jamā'at al-Tawḥīd wa-al-Jihād (literally translated as 'The Organization of Monotheism and Jihad') proclaimed themselves a caliphate, with authority and leadership over the entire Muslim world. They would later become known as ISIS, and later still, as Islamic State, and within a decade commit some of the most horrific atrocities of the twenty-first century.

In October 2003, however, ISIS were just another of the myriad terrorist groups flooding Iraq with fighters and weapons. Emerging leaders, many of whom had travelled to Iraq purely to wage jihad, were now a greater danger than the remnants of the old government; and identifying, finding and eliminating them became the new priority.

Towards the end of that month, US intelligence intercepted communications from a known Sudanese jihadist instrumental in smuggling Islamist militants into Iraq. By tracking the signals, they were able to identify his location precisely: a compound of buildings on the edge of the city of Ramadi, 70 miles (113 km) west of the capital along the Baghdad Highway.

This wasn't a former politician fleeing to Syria or an ex-general hiding in the desert; this was a functioning operational threat, actively working to destabilize the fragile peace and endanger the lives of British and American troops. Taking him out – and whatever terrorists he was harbouring in his compound – was imperative.

The intelligence was sound, but the operation itself had to be handled delicately. Ramadi was a volatile city and a hotbed of insurgency, with bomb attacks and ambushes on coalition forces commonplace. The compound would certainly be defended; what was unknown was just how strongly, and what further spontaneous resistance might be faced once the assault began.

American command took the decision that storming the compound was too great a job for Delta Force to handle alone. Twenty-four men from SAS 'A' Squadron would join them, and just in case things went badly wrong, both units would be backed up by a platoon of M2 Bradley heavy armoured vehicles: fast, highly manoeuvrable, and armed with 25-mm (1-inch) machine-gun cannons and anti-tank missile launchers, the Bradleys would be kept in reserve until called upon.

The operation was given the codename Abalone.

Time was short and the opportunity for detailed reconnaissance limited. The basic details seemed fairly straightforward, however. The compound was made up of a collection of houses in a dusty yard on the edge of town, protected by a high fence with metal gates. Other houses bordered them, but intelligence indicated that only the four in the main compound were to be considered a threat.

The British and US forces divided the buildings between them: Delta Force would take two, the SAS would handle the remaining two. If the signal was given, the Bradleys would open up with their 25-mms and anti-tank rockets on any or all of them.

On the night of 31 October, as children in America and the UK dressed as monsters and devils for Halloween, the men of Operation Abalone were about to experience real terror.

◆ ◆ ◆

Initially at least, things went well. The two Delta Force squads took their buildings free from incident, finding them both apparently deserted. At the same time, the first twelve-man SAS unit entered their building. Decades of experience combating urban-based terrorism during the Troubles in Northern Ireland had made the SAS unmatched in quickly securing even unfamiliar buildings: now, moving along a pattern practised so often it had become second nature, as instinctive and automatic as squeezing a trigger, two-man teams cleared the house room by room, cover and move, move and cover, fast and efficient and ready to be deadly.

They, too, found no resistance. Where was the enemy?

The answer was not long in coming.

As the second SAS unit ran through the gates towards their building, the yard exploded in a storm of light and noise. Two men sustained serious injuries, as well as the two who did not make it back out of the compound.

There was no question of bringing the Bradleys' big guns to bear while any SAS man might still be alive in there. That one was dead seemed a grim certainty, but the other was not only clearly still alive, but apparently also still prepared to fight.

The men sent to investigate didn't hesitate.

Acting as one, the troopers sprinted across the yard that had only minutes before been a maelstrom of bullets. Miraculously, their approach hadn't been noticed – the defenders inside must have presumed no one would be insane enough to attempt another attack so soon – but with the fallen man so close to the very windows from which the guns had been fired, it was only a matter of time.

Sure enough, as they grabbed him under his arms, hauled him to his feet and began dragging him back to safety, a shout went up from inside the building. Once again, the silence was shattered by the guttural stammer and bark of AK-47 fire, and the ground around them kicked and spat with bullets.

Somehow they made it without further injury. Back behind the gates, as medics attended to the wounded men, the order was given to the Bradleys, and the terrorists inside the compound got a taste of their own medicine.

A barrage of gunfire and anti-tank rockets smashed into the building, concrete and masonry shattering and splintering, walls collapsing, windows blowing. The moment the bombardment stopped, Delta Force stormed in, backed up with covering fire from the first SAS team on the roofs of the three buildings already secured.

By the time the US special forces men penetrated the building, little remained of it but a shell. Everyone inside was dead, most buried under so much rubble that identifying even how many there were was all but impossible.

Meanwhile, all the gunfire and explosions had not gone unnoticed. Shots came from a fifth, unaccounted-for building, targeting the SAS troops on the roofs of the secured compound houses.

For the third time that night, the SAS stormed a hostile building. Once inside, it became clear that this was no ordinary suburban residence: rooms were filthy and unkempt, littered with detritus, spent ammunition and jihadist literature espousing death and vengeance to the Western infidels.

The defenders were efficiently dealt with. One was killed as he fired his AK-47, four others were taken prisoner.

And still, the fighting was not done. As the Delta Force and SAS teams emerged from the five secured buildings, the locals were getting involved too. Sporadic small-arms fire popped and whistled from other buildings and along the streets. Increasingly angry shouts grew in number and volume. Petrol bombs skidded and exploded.

The situation was close to getting out of hand, degenerating into an all-out riot on the streets of Ramadi – precisely the kind of confrontation that could forever shatter the fragile, uneasy authority the coalition forces held over the city.

Instead of properly securing the scene, tallying the dead terrorists and searching to see if the original Sudanese jihadist target was among them, the special forces made the call to pull out.

Two SAS troopers ran into the compound to retrieve their fallen colleague, now definitely confirmed as dead, and helicopters were called in to evacuate both him and the injured men to the hospital at the nearby US base. The rest loaded into Land Rovers and the Bradleys and sped away, the compound smouldering behind them, gunfire following their exit.

◆ ◆ ◆

Operation Abalone was one of the first genuinely joint operations between Delta Force and the SAS, and was pronounced a success. Although the lack of a proper examination of the battleground meant it was impossible to confirm whether the prime objective had been achieved, interrogation of the four prisoners taken by the SAS revealed that they were non-Iraqi nationals newly arrived from the Yemen and Saudi Arabia, proving that Iraq had become a destination for international jihadists.

As well as those four prisoners, as many as a dozen insurgents are suspected to have been killed in the battle, for the loss of just one man.

Corporal Ian Plank, from Poole in Dorset, was a Royal Marine from the Special Boat Service who had been attached to the SAS. He had been shot through the head as his squad stormed the compound. He was thirty-one years old when he died and the first British special forces soldier to be killed in the Iraq War.

In a statement to the press on 4 November 2003, Colonel Jerry Heal of the Royal Marines said: 'Ian Plank ... was particularly well known for his resilience and robustness under pressure, when his leadership, example and sense of humour were especially valued. He enriched the lives of those who knew him, both socially and in the workplace. His positive outlook, bright disposition and zest for life will be remembered with deep pride and affection by all those who knew him.'

OPERATION MARLBOROUGH

IRAQ, 23 JULY 2005

THEY CALLED THEM 'Task Force Black'. The elite of the elite British and American special forces troops in Iraq, put together specifically to take down terrorists in clandestine search-and-destroy missions. Made up of a squadron of SAS troopers along with members of Delta Force, as well as men from the SBS and US Navy Seals, they also went by a more informal nickname: the hunter-killers.

The 'black' in Task Force Black referred to the covert, hidden nature of their operations: working with a network of Iraqi spies placed, turned and cultivated by the CIA and MI6, their missions were classified at the highest level. Even today, the troopers of Task Force Black remain anonymous, their identities and activities concealed not only in the interests of national security, but also for their own protection. Jihad does not come with a statute of limitations, and fanatics have long and bitter memories.

Operations were not only top secret, but also mostly conducted at extremely short notice. The very nature of the live intelligence they worked from – and the kind of enemy they were now fighting – meant that the opportunity to act decisively had to be taken immediately as it was presented.

Time was of the essence. Mistakes were a luxury they could not afford.

This was never more true than when chasing down suicide bombers. This most basic and brutal of terrorist tactics – when a wannabe martyr would strap a vest loaded with explosives around themselves to be self-detonated in a location deliberately picked to cause as many casualties and as much devastation as possible – had become the fundamentalist terror groups' weapon of choice. One person's sacrifice could kill or maim scores, even hundreds, of infidels, and assure the bomber a guaranteed place in Paradise into the bargain. Win-win for the fundamentalists.

As terror groups led by al-Qaeda flooded post-war Iraq, suicide bombers became ever-more prevalent. From 2004, in the big cities and coalition strongholds like Baghdad, Mosul, Basra, Erbil and Ramadi, such attacks wreaked devastation … and the terrorists were not only targeting Westerners.

In February 2004, 117 people were killed by two suicide bombers in Erbil as crowds gathered to celebrate Eid; the following month, at least 180 Shi'ite Muslims were killed in a series of suicide bombings in Baghdad and Karbala, among them forty-nine Iranian pilgrims come to celebrate the Islamic festival of Ashura.

In April, five terrorists driving cars loaded with explosives blew themselves up near police stations in Basra, killing seventy-four, including eighteen schoolchildren, and injuring 160 others. Another sixty-eight Iraqis were killed by a man wearing an explosive vest as they queued outside a Baqubah police recruiting centre in July; and in September, suicide bombers targeting US soldiers handing out sweets in Baghdad killed thirty-five children and wounded a further seventy-two under the age of fourteen. In December, a self-proclaimed martyr targeted a funeral procession in Najaf, claiming at least fifty more victims.

By 2005, suicide bombers were endemic in Iraq: in the first six months of the year alone, at least forty-seven significant suicide bomb attacks were recorded – the equivalent of about two a week, every week.

These attacks were not only a simple and horribly effective means of spreading terror and devastation, they also required little in the way of complicated planning. Once the basic materials – and a willing believer – had been acquired, all that was necessary was to decide upon a location.

For the men of Task Force Black this meant that most of their operations to combat them were conducted within a tiny window of opportunity – often barely a few days between receiving intelligence of a planned attack and neutralizing the threat.

In late July 2005 came one such opportunity. Double-agents run by MI6 had come through with intelligence of a planned triple suicide bomb attack in the heart of the Iraq capital. Three al-Qaeda insurgents were holed up in a house in southern Baghdad: on the morning of 23 July they were going to split up and head to the busiest parts of the city, where they would detonate their devices in cafes, markets or other areas targeted to cause the maximum number of civilian casualties.

The spies were firm in their conviction. The threat was clear and present. But they had managed to plant listening devices inside the house, meaning that Coalition Command would be able to hear the terrorists as they prepared to carry out their attack.

Task Force Black was immediately engaged.

The operation was assigned to a joint force from 'M' Squadron SBS and 'G' Squadron, 22 SAS. Sixteen men were divided into four sniper units, each made up of a shooter and a spotter, with the remaining eight troopers providing cover and security for the sniper teams. In addition, a further platoon of US Army Rangers remained close at hand, and above them all, 2,000 feet (610 m) high in the skies, a CIA Predator drone would oversee the whole area, beaming live images back to Command HQ.

In the hour before dawn on 23 July, Task Force Black, given the operational name Marlborough, swung silently into action.

◆ ◆ ◆

The two-man sniper units edged across the rooftops and along the deserted street in darkness, all in black and with balaclavas covering their faces. One man from each team carried an L115A1 bolt-action sniper rifle – in the right hands, capable of firing with devastating accuracy from a range of 1,500 metres (1,640 yards). In the chambers were .338 Lapua Magnum cartridges, the biggest and most powerful bullet used by the British army, able to penetrate all but the highest-grade body armour.

For the previous twenty-four hours' detailed satellite images of the area around the house had been studied until every crack in the pavement and chip in the stone walls was seared into the troopers' brains; they moved with absolute certainty, knowing almost without looking exactly where they were to go.

Working almost invisibly and in absolute silence, they each took positions some 250 metres (273 yards) from the al-Qaeda safe house, under cover but with a clear sight of the entrance to the building. The rifles were rested on their mounts, the sights trained, and the front of the house zoomed into view. A further four troopers moved into covering positions around them, watching their backs, wary of an ambush or trap. Intelligence had been wrong before, and the SAS knew from hard-fought experience that the problem with trusting in double-agents was ... they were double-agents.

If the intel was to be trusted, then the three suspects would exit from the front door, bomb vests hidden under their clothes, looking for all the world like any other Baghdad citizens heading to work in the rush hour. If the intel was to be trusted.

Just in case, the final four men covered the rear of the building, watching for runners attempting to exit that way.

Further backup came from the nearby – though out of sight – Army Rangers, and just minutes away were RAF Puma helicopters carrying further snipers. Both forces were to stay clear unless needed: an obvious show of strength in the area might spook the bombers and spark a disaster.

Bomb vests explode in messy, unpredictable ways; the team had no way of knowing just how much explosive the men might be carrying, or what potentially deadly shrapnel they might also be loaded with. Rucksacks and pockets filled with nails could increase the lethal effect of a suicide bomb to a horrific extent.

Plus there was the danger of the bombers detonating themselves in the house itself. How much other explosive might be stored there? In such a confined space any blast would be massively amplified, destroying most of the street and almost certainly killing or seriously injuring anyone on or around it.

It was for this reason that the decision to use snipers was made. Storming the building in a traditional cover-and-move formation, as the SAS had done in Operation Abalone, was simply too risky. It only took a moment for a suicide bomber to trigger his vest; the targets had to be eliminated literally before they knew what hit them.

The orders were unequivocal. Let the bombers exit and move clear of the building. Wait until the command to shoot. Headshots to each of them. All three to be hit simultaneously. No room for error.

Each of the three two-man sniper teams were assigned a bomber to eliminate; the fourth unit would cover all three, in the (unlikely) event one of the shots failed to hit its target. Earpiece commentary relayed from Arabic translators listening in to events inside the house would confirm exactly when the jihadists were preparing to move, and when to take them down.

At a little after 08.00 hours, as the morning sun warmed the streets and rooftops of suburban Baghdad and the task force troopers began to sweat inside their balaclavas, finally, a voice in their ears: 'Stand by. Stand by.'

The intel was good. The bombers were preparing to leave the safe house by the front door. Spotters trained their binoculars; lying beside them, the snipers put their eyes to the sights on their rifles, their fingers light on the triggers, concentrating on the moment, and the moment alone.

The door opened, and three men, casually dressed if a little bulky looking, stepped into the sunlight, separating into clear, distinct targets in the July sunlight. Again, the earpieces came to life, the voice calm and unambiguous: 'Engage.'

From 250 metres away, three index fingers squeezed in precise synchronicity, and three high-velocity, armour-piercing bullets flew at nearly 1,000 metres (1,093 yards) per second towards their targets.

At the same time, the waiting Puma helicopters were engaged, speeding towards the battle, their own shooters ready to eliminate any threats missed by the ground force.

Opinions differ about what happened next. According to some accounts, in the quarter of a second between the bullet leaving the barrel of the L115A1 rifle and penetrating his skull, one of the bombers managed to detonate his vest. Mercifully far enough away from the houses and the SAS men not to kill anyone but himself, the shockwaves of his blast nonetheless sent the Puma directly overhead into a dangerous tilt and spin. As the helicopter reeled and pitched, the pilot somehow managed to regain control, pulling up just metres above the houses and narrowly avoiding disaster.

Other accounts are less dramatic. By their telling, each of the three snipers found their targets with true and deadly accuracy, the .338 Lapua Magnum cartridges striking with lethal effect, killing the would-be bombers instantly.

Either way, the threat was immobilized, with no civilian or military casualties – and on the street lay three would-be jihadi martyrs, eliminated before they could murder anyone but themselves.

The snipers withdrew, and the main force moved in to the house. The danger was not yet over – three bombers were known of and removed, but other al-Qaeda operatives could remain inside, along with an unknown amount of weapons and explosives.

Cover and move. Room by room, the men of Task Force Black secured the building. The house was mercifully empty: no further terrorists were found, although a large cache of explosives, fuses, triggers and other bomb vest components were uncovered – presumably for the next influx of fanatics prepared to blow themselves up in the name of holy war. Bomb disposal experts were called in, and the special forces men left them to it.

Operation Marlborough was a rare and precious success against the epidemic of suicide bombers in post-invasion Iraq. It may have only been three men removed, but the combined damage they were intent on causing could have killed hundreds of innocent Iraqi men, women and children. Against such a flood of hatred, every life saved was a victory.

BASRA PRISON RAID

IRAQ, 19 SEPTEMBER 2005

THE LIEUTENANT COLONEL thought long and hard before he spoke. The next words he chose could cost him his career, or they could condemn two of his men to possible torture and even death. In the end, it was no choice at all.

He spoke, and put the phone down. Minutes later, a Hercules transport plane containing twenty members of 'A' Squadron, 22 SAS, along with a platoon of paratroopers from the Special Forces Support Group, took off from Baghdad, heading 300 miles (483 km) south, to Basra.

There they would join the already emplaced SAS squadron in launching a direct assault on the city's police station, possibly, it might be conceded, in defiance of the direct instruction of the British government itself.

◆ ◆ ◆

Ever since Paddy Mayne kicked in the door of the officers' mess at Tamet airfield in 1941 and announced a new means of waging war, the SAS had done things differently. Although still a part of the British Armed Forces, and as such subject to the protocols and chains of command integral to order and discipline in the army, it had nonetheless been born out of a desire to break convention, from the start a band of rogue heroes, willing to rewrite the rule book if that's what it took to get the job done. It did things its own way. The SAS way.

The SAS was not exactly a law unto itself, though sometimes it could seem that way.

The lieutenant colonel's problems had begun that morning. Two of his men had been operating deep undercover, working to expose corruption and brutality in the Basra police force. Disguised as Iraqi civilians, complete with fake tan and hair dye, they had been tailing a senior police officer from a borrowed taxi when other policemen challenged them.

A scuffle broke out, punches were thrown, the officers drew their weapons ... but the commandos drew theirs first. At least two Iraqi policemen were shot – some reports say fatally, though this has never been confirmed – and the SAS men dived back into their car and floored the pedal, tyres squealing as they raced away to a safe rendezvous point.

Hyper-alert to militant gun attacks after two years of rising tensions in the city, the Basra police gave chase. Roadblocks were set up, reinforcements radioed in, and with every turn the fleeing commandos were forced to take to avoid them, they were diverted further from the safety of the emergency RV point.

Realizing that escape was impossible, and in an attempt to de-escalate the situation before it blew up into a major incident, they stopped the car, threw away their weapons and emerged slowly, hands up. Once the police were given the full facts, they reasoned, and understood they were British army, they were confident they could talk themselves out of further trouble.

'British,' they called, as the officers advanced upon them. 'British army. British army officers.'

The policemen didn't understand them, didn't believe them, or didn't care either way. Their legs kicked out from beneath them, the two SAS men were handcuffed as they hit the ground, then beaten with fists, batons and gun butts, before being slung into the back of a van and taken to the cells at Al Jameat police station for interrogation.

As far as the Basra police were concerned, their actions were more than justified. Two armed and dangerous men guilty of shooting police officers had been detained, and now they deserved all they got.

The police went further: they claimed the captured men were assassins and agent provocateurs, that their shooting of the officers had been unprovoked and in cold blood, and that their mission was to sabotage the fragile peace and even plant bombs to create a 'false flag' terrorist attack. Trumpeting the men's arrest as a victory for law and order, they even broadcast images of their prisoners, bruised, bandaged and bloodied from further beatings, in their cells.

For the SAS commanding officer, there was no question of leaving his men in there. The scale of corruption in the Basra police force meant they were at risk of being turned over to one of the extremist militia groups, who would pay well for the chance to parade the corpses of two British special forces men as trophies.

Negotiations began to secure the release of the men, but the talks broke down immediately: the police simply would not budge.

It seemed there was no other option. If the Basra police wouldn't release them peacefully, then the SAS would have to go in and get them out themselves, by whatever means necessary.

And they'd better be sharp about it: with every hour that passed, the chances of the prisoners surviving grew slimmer.

Every special forces man in Basra was put on high readiness – and reinforcements called in from 'A' Squadron in Baghdad, as well as the Support Group Paras.

And then, even as the troops boarded the Hercules for the flight to Basra, came a call from the Ministry of Defence, patched through all the way from London.

It was not the message the lieutenant colonel was expecting.

The situation was a little more delicate than the SAS appreciated, he was told. The government felt it was important to understand the bigger picture, and how such an operation might affect public perception of the British forces' role in Iraq. Perhaps the real issue here was not the welfare of two special forces men who had anyway trained for years to withstand the kind of rough treatment they were probably getting from their captors, but how attacking an Iraqi police station might undermine Basra's image as a city where the British were successfully handing power and authority back to the Iraqi people. The political position was precarious, he was told. Didn't he agree it shouldn't be jeopardized for the sake of a couple of commandos? Wouldn't those reinforcements about to depart Baghdad be better deployed on more useful missions?

The lieutenant colonel had hung up without answering, astonished and enraged by what he had just heard. He hadn't exactly received a direct order to stand the rescue operation down, but the inference couldn't be clearer. It seemed the British government wanted him to effectively sacrifice two of his troopers for the sake of a bit of political PR.

He ran through his options. As far as he could tell, he had three choices.

First: do as his superiors back in Whitehall suggested and abandon his men – potentially to the same kind of horrors faced by the soldiers of Bravo Two Zero, and likely even worse.

Unthinkable.

Second: resign in protest.

Pointless.

Third: do whatever it took to bring his men home and bugger the politicians.

That was the Paddy Mayne way, the David Stirling way. The SAS way.

He picked up the phone again.

We go anyway.

Who dares wins.

◆ ◆ ◆

If the SAS were going to do this, then they were going all-in. As afternoon faded into evening, they came to Al Jameat police station in numbers, and in force. Tanks and Armoured Personnel Vehicles thundered through the streets, supported by the Basra SAS troopers and their Baghdad reinforcements, as well as a squad of infantrymen from the Staffordshire Regiment. Overhead, a Predator drone and Lynx helicopter buzzed the skies.

Their presence had not gone unnoticed. Quite the reverse – Iraqi television had been broadcasting the images of the British prisoners all afternoon, and throughout the day a crowd had grown around the jail. By the time the SAS rescue force turned up, they were hundreds strong, and shot through with numerous militants intent on causing trouble.

As the tanks and APVs formed a protective circle around the station, it began.

The British were intent on trying one last time to resolve the situation peacefully. Two officers from the 12th Armoured Brigade approached the jail with a letter of ultimatum: release the SAS men, or face the consequences.

The Iraqi officers let them in ... but would not let them out again. There were now four British soldiers prisoner inside, and the window for negotiation was well and truly over.

At the same time, tensions in the crowd boiled over. Someone threw a stone towards the British cordon; it was followed by another, then another ... and then a Molotov cocktail came corkscrewing, a glass bottle full of petrol, burning rag stuffed into the neck. It smashed on impact with one of the APVs, sending a blinding sheet of flame up and over the vehicle.

It was like a dam bursting: suddenly the air was thick with improvised missiles, a deadly hailstorm of rock and gasoline and fire. One of the personnel vehicles was fatally hit, the men inside scrambling to free themselves from being burned alive. Added to the chaos came gunfire, as insurgents and al-Qaeda militants in the crowd seized the chance to inflict more casualties on the British forces.

And then another complication: through the bedlam a car came screaming out of the station, through the barricade and into the darkened streets. Footage from the Predator drone monitoring events back to HQ suggested that the two SAS men had been bundled into the back and were being taken to an al-Qaeda safe house on the outskirts of the city.

Enough was enough. With two APVs now burning, four men taken hostage, and the mob outside the station increasingly murderous, it was time to regain some control.

'A' Squadron SAS, along with the men from the Staffordshire Regiment and all of the armoured vehicles, would storm the prison; the rest of the force would follow the intel from the drone to the location where the original SAS prisoners had been taken and attempt to secure their rescue with immediate effect. At that moment, the primary concern was reaching them before they were executed.

As the Lynx made repeated low passes over the crowd, infantrymen stemmed the riot with controlled bursts of automatic fire. Two Iraqi protestors fell under shrapnel and ricochets, the rest drew back. At the same time, the remaining APVs advanced into the mob and tanks rolled towards the station itself, bulldozing through the flimsy perimeter, crashing through the prison walls, bricks and concrete and plaster crumbling and crushed under them.

The building may have served as an adequate police station and prison, but it was not built to withstand an assault from a tank brigade. Warrior and Challenger tanks made short work of the structure: within minutes the former stronghold was reduced to rubble.

Resistance inside had fled. There was no answering fire, only the scurrying bodies of escaping prisoners. Two who didn't run were the men from the 12th Armoured Brigade: with a grin and a grimace, they were hoisted into the vehicles unharmed.

Meanwhile, the rest of the force had followed the drone to a house in the suburbs where the two SAS men had been taken.

Things here were calmer, and the squadron were able to move with practised efficiency.

On a signal, front and rear doors were smashed; further two-man teams entered through windows. Rooms were secured, the men moved on without incident. Finally, without encountering a single enemy, they found the hostages, handcuffed in a locked room, beaten and bloodied, but otherwise sound.

Whether they had been abandoned or Islamist militants planned to return to deal with them later will never be known.

◆ ◆ ◆

The aftermath of the Basra prison rescue would resonate for years. The whole operation was conducted under the glare of rolling news coverage. Images of the SAS prisoners inside Al Jameat police station had been broadcast on Iraqi television and were quickly picked up by international networks. Press Association cameras and amateur footage had also captured the chaos outside the prison as the British prepared to storm the building: one image especially – of a burning soldier scrambling to safety from a petrol-bombed APV – made headlines worldwide.

Nevertheless, the bottom line was irrefutable: all British military personnel had been rescued alive and (relatively) unharmed. The SAS had not been prepared to give up any of their men. The Lieutenant Colonel's call to 'go anyway' had been vindicated.

Back in Whitehall, the reaction was less enthusiastic. In the immediate aftermath of the operation, the Ministry of Defence first said that the SAS men had been released through negotiations and denied any storming of the prison had taken place, before later conceding that a 'wall' may have been accidentally de-molished as British forces tried to 'collect' the prisoners.

For the lieutenant colonel who put his career on the line to save two of his men, the government's reaction was as much – and perhaps more – than he could expect. Retrospective authority for the rescue was eventually given, but he was under no illusions that had things turned out less favourably then the verdict on his decision to defy government advice would have been very different.

Such was the SAS. Not exactly a law unto itself ... though sometimes it could seem that way.

OPERATION LIGHTWATER AND THE RESCUE OF NORMAN KEMBER

IRAQ, 23 MARCH 2006

THEY WERE IN IRAQ to spread a message of peace and non-violent conflict resolution; documenting human-rights abuses and publicly condemning what they described as the 'illegal occupation' of the country. Formed shortly before the first Gulf War, they were a Christian organization formed mostly of Quakers and Baptists, but embracing a multi-cultural, religiously diverse philosophy that placed tolerance and acceptance above all else.

However, British professor Norman Kember, 74, Canadians James Loney, 41, and Harmeet Singh Sooden, 32, together with American Tom Fox, 54, of aid agency the Christian Peacemakers, had been held hostage for months by an Islamist fundamentalist cell styling themselves 'The Swords of Righteousness Brigade'.

Snatched as they travelled to an appointment with the Muslim Clerics Association at a mosque in central Baghdad, the peace activists had been bundled into a car at gunpoint by men in balaclavas wielding AK-47s, and taken to a safe house, where they were told they would be killed if their captors' demands were not met.

That was on 26 November 2005. After nearly four months of captivity, on 10 March 2006, the threat was made horribly real.

The body of Tom Fox was found dumped in the west of the city. He had been shot in the head and chest. His hands and feet were still tied, and his body showed signs of torture.

And still, despite their trauma, even the murder of one of their own, the three remaining British and Canadian hostages stuck to their pacifist ideals: they did not want to be rescued if that was to involve violence. On grainy videos released by their kidnappers and broadcast on Arab satellite channel Al Jazeera, they repeated their stance: while they condemned their capture, they rejected violence as a punishment for anyone, even their captors.

It was certainly a principle worthy of respect. But with one innocent man already killed and the fate of the other three hanging in the balance, such idealism was also a luxury that looked increasingly unaffordable.

The SAS were hunting for them, and they were prepared to do whatever it took to save them. Whether the Christian Peacemakers approved or not.

◆ ◆ ◆

In the three years after the invasion of Iraq, more than 200 non-Iraqi citizens had been kidnapped by radical militia groups – of those, fifty-four had not survived their ordeal.

That works out as an average of three foreign nationals taken hostage every two weeks; and the murder of a foreign hostage roughly once every three weeks. These were bone-chilling statistics, and especially uncomfortable for a coalition campaign that had promised to bring peace and stability to the region.

Once again, Task Force Black – now called Task Force Knight after the original codename had been leaked to the media – were assigned to combat the threat. From suicide bombers, they turned their attention to kidnappers, though in reality it wasn't too great a leap: if one were to draw a Venn diagram of al-Qaeda operations in mid-2000s Iraq, the crossover between the two would be by far the most significant part of the equation.

Working once more with the men of Delta Force, they put a new operation into action.

Operation Lightwater was a collaboration between US and UK special forces in which the bulk of intelligence was supplied by the Americans and the majority of muscle by the British. The stated aim was the recovery of British national Norman Kember and the other Christian Peacemaker hostages – in reality, it was a coordinated and ruthless campaign against all suspected al-Qaeda operatives in Iraq.

◆ ◆ ◆

After the four Westerners had been kidnapped, The Swords of Righteousness Brigade didn't waste time in making their demands heard. Three days after the men's disappearance, a video was released on the Al Jazeera network. It showed the four hostages wearing orange jumpsuits – a reference to the prisoners held at Guantanamo Bay by the Americans – while one of the kidnappers decried them as spies. They also made a demand, and set a deadline: unless all Iraqi prisoners held in both the US and Iraq were freed by 8 December, the four peace workers would be executed.

Even more chillingly, two of the men, Tom Fox and Norman Kember, were blindfolded and their hands chained. Both were also prompted to make statements in which they not only begged their governments to assist in their release, but also appealed for the liberation of, in Kember's words, 'all the people of Iraq', adding: 'The only way that we can all be free is for the American and British soldiers to leave Iraq as soon as possible.'

It did not escape notice that, of the four prisoners, it was only the American and British men who were chained and blindfolded.

The response of the British and US governments was unequivocal. They were open to negotiation, they said, but the group's demands, in the words of British Foreign Minister Jack Straw, speaking to reporters, were of a scale that 'plainly, no government could meet'.

The deadline was extended by two days; again there was no progress. And then, for a month, there was silence.

In the meantime, the kidnapping had become front-page news worldwide, with – unusually for such incidents in Iraq – condemnation coming from almost across the board. The nature of the Christian Peacemakers' work, and the fact that they had been opposed to the war from the beginning, meant that even for some Islamist extremists, they did not represent a 'fair' target.

Pleas for their release came even from prominent radical Muslim leaders such as Abu Qatada, the high-profile Islamist described as Osama bin Laden's ambassador in Britain. The kidnappers ignored them. Another video was released at the end of January 2006, in which all four hostages were shown to be alive and the captors offered 'one last chance' for their demands to be met ... and then silence once again.

On 7 March came the final video. This time there was no audio, and no sign of the terrorists; it simply showed Norman Kember, James Loney and Harmeet Singh Sooden sitting at a table, with a timestamp of 28 February.

The fourth hostage, American Tom Fox, was nowhere to be seen.

◆ ◆ ◆

Although to the outside world it may have looked like the British and American governments had been content to call the kidnappers' bluff for the four months since the capture of the Christian Peacemakers, on the ground an urgent and clandestine special forces operation had been working furiously to find the hostages.

Operation Lightwater was to be a new way of combating the deadly rash of kidnappings and other terrorist activity. Rather than using traditional methods of regular patrols, shows of strength on the streets and emplaced double-agents, Delta Force and the SAS instead used the emerging drone, GPS and mobile phone technologies to build a vast web of information on any and all suspects.

Knowledge is power. All known Islamist extremists, as well as their families, associates, associates of their families, suspected associates, associates of associates, and anyone else with any kind of connection to them, were placed under twenty-four-hour surveillance by a fleet of unmanned Predator drones that patrolled the skies above Baghdad. Their every movement was tracked, their every action monitored, and armed with this information, updated in real time by troopers in a dedicated control room, the men of Lightwater embarked on a series of lightning raids across the city.

Delta Force supplied the intelligence and the target locations, 'B' Squadron, 22 SAS did the dirty work. Throughout the late winter of 2006, almost every night saw another house swooped upon by the SAS, its occupants hauled in for immediate interrogation, questioned relentlessly while they were still reeling from their capture, their confusion meaning they would often be more likely to give up names, addresses and other information before they had time to recover.

It was an operation where the intelligence expanded almost exponentially – with every suspect questioned, the web of targets grew greater, as further associates, especially through mobile phone records, were uncovered. They were targeted in turn, which led to still further intelligence, until trackers were put on almost every suspected terrorist cell and al-Qaeda operative in Baghdad.

It was like a storm sweeping through the city, suspects surprised at gunpoint in their own homes without warning, completely unaware that invisible eyes had been monitoring their every movement, hidden watchers tracking their every text and phone call.

In a little over two months, Operation Lightwater raided no fewer than fifty separate locations and detained forty-seven people. Only four of those raids failed to turn up information that led to the confiscation of weapons, bomb-making equipment, jihadist propaganda materials or further targets.

Shortly after midnight on 23 March, just two weeks after the body of Tom Fox had been found, and with concern growing over the fate of the other hostages – Briton Norman Kember especially – Lightwater's unique fusion of cutting-edge technology and in-your-face power finally blew the search for the Christian Peacemakers wide open.

The pattern of suspects and their associates had led to a raid on a house in the town of Mishahda, 20 miles (32 km) north of Baghdad. As usual, the SAS team that burst into the building caught the two occupants by surprise, and they were whisked away for interrogation before other nearby residents even knew the raid had happened at all.

Under what was later described as 'pressure' questioning, one of the men gave up the information the SAS had been seeking since November: an address in west Baghdad where Norman Kember, James Loney and Harmeet Singh Sooden were being held.

There was no time to lose. An assault force was put together within the hour, and before dawn had broken over Baghdad they were moving in on the house. A team from 'B' Squadron SAS was to spearhead the assault, with a support unit of paratroopers and marines, plus members of the Royal Canadian Mounted Police, on hand if needed.

Norman Kember and the other members of the Christian Peacemakers had been adamant – even despite the killing of Tom Fox – that any rescue should be performed by entirely non-violent means; but although the SAS respected that stance in theory, in practice it could go to hell. They were fighting vicious, fanatical murderers, and they were doing so with every weapon at their disposal.

As they waited for the 'Go' order, every man was ready to do whatever it took to get those hostages out alive.

But despite the urgency, the SAS were not about to rush the house blind. Three years battling terrorist cells in Iraq, and two months of near-nightly raids on al-Qaeda-held buildings during Operation Lightwater, had made them smarter than that. The vast network of information built up on militant Islamist activity in Baghdad had led them to this point ... but, ultimately, the address was still the word of just one informant.

After losing Corporal Ian Plank in Operation Abalone, they did not want to walk into another trap. And that's when one of the officers had a flash of inspiration.

Thanks to the mobile phone records of the men they had just brought in, they not only had an address for the kidnap location, they also had a phone number for the kidnappers. In an outrageous double-bluff, a call was put in to the terrorists directly.

The SAS are coming for you, they were told. Best make yourselves scarce. The men on their way aren't quite so keen on non-violent conflict resolution as your captives.

At 08.00 hours the SAS squad moved in. Bursting through front and back doors simultaneously as other teams covered the windows, they moved fast through the rooms, clearing each in turn. Finally, they smashed through the locks of the last room in the building. There, sitting calmly, were all three hostages.

The pre-emptive phone call had been a masterstroke. Knowing the game was up and that any battle against the SAS was only going to have one outcome, the terrorists had fled.

As it turned out, that moment of inspiration had not only secured the release of the three men, but done so without a shot being fired, just as the Christian Peacemakers had wanted all along.

◆ ◆ ◆

The rescue of Norman Kember, James Loney and Harmeet Singh Sooden was an unqualified success, and a vindication of the vast anti-terrorism surveillance network that Operation Lightwater had pioneered.

In the aftermath of the rescue, not everyone was quite so jubilant, however. The Christian Peacemakers' original statement was muted in its praise of the SAS, only expressing gratitude that no one had been hurt in the operation, and Norman Kember himself came under prolonged criticism for his initial failure to thank the men who had risked their lives to save him.

Six months later, another raid finally caught the kidnappers. Once again, Kember refused to compromise his pacifist ideals and declined to testify at the trial of the men who had kept him prisoner for 118 days.

OPERATION LARCHWOOD 4

IRAQ, 16 APRIL 2006

THE PUMA LANDED shortly after 02.00 hours on the edge of the orchard and its force of commandos melted into the trees in absolute silence. At the same time, a platoon of British Paras from the Special Forces Support Group first formed in Operation Barras six years before, unloaded from Chinooks a short distance away and took up positions around the perimeter of the farm, settling in under cover, watching intently. Nobody would get close to – or escape from – the area without their say-so.

Above them all, Lynx helicopters whirred through the skies; inside, SAS snipers trained their night sights and waited.

As they ghosted through the trees, the assault force split into two units, one continuing directly eastwards towards the target buildings, the other skirting around to the south. As they reached the edge of the orchard, both teams paused, waited, watched.

The farm was on an isolated patch of land just outside the town of Yusufiyah, around 10 miles (16 km) from Baghdad's southern suburbs. A scattering of ramshackle outbuildings surrounded the large main house. They had already been secured as clear; now all attention was focused on the central building itself.

All looked quiet, calm, exactly as one might expect at two in the morning. The house was dark and still, a black and inscrutable silhouette. The only sound was the intermittent creak of an unlocked door swinging slowly back and forth on its hinges, caught by the gentle breeze of a cool April night.

And still the SAS teams waited. Intelligence gathered from raids the previous week, combined and confirmed with mobile phone intercepts and drone reconnaissance, indicated that inside that building was an al-Qaeda leader and one of the terrorist organization's key propaganda heads. He would not be alone, and he would not want to come quietly.

Finally, a signal was given and two commandos crept forward towards the south-east corner of the building, and the unlocked door. Still nothing moved inside the house; all remained dark, silent.

The scouts took up positions either side of the door, and as a team of troopers emerged from the trees and moved through it, fell in behind them. The raid was on.

They barely made a few steps inside before the shooting started.

◆ ◆ ◆

The Americans called it 'The Triangle of Death' – and for good reason, too.

A poor, mostly rural area south of Baghdad bordered by the River Euphrates to the south-west, it was home to around 1 million Iraqis, and a hotbed of violence and anti-Western extremism. Suicide and car bombings were commonplace – and so too were direct assaults on US and British patrols that were marked not only by their audacity, but also by their extreme viciousness. In one incident, three American soldiers had been kidnapped near Jurf Al Sakhar – their remains were found four days later close to their base: their bodies had been mutilated, dismembered, burned and beheaded, as well as booby-trapped with improvised explosive devices hidden between their legs.

The coalition may have kidded themselves they were in charge in Iraq, but in the spring of 2006, the Triangle of Death was a brutal, lawless zone in which radical militant groups like al-Qaeda held more real power and authority on the ground than any Western forces.

It was into this febrile, intensely hostile atmosphere that the SAS were launching their raid on the farmhouse south of Yusufiyah. They were after an al-Qaeda figurehead, a key player in terrorist attacks in the Triangle of Death area, and one of the most prolific propagandists for the organization in all Iraq. Not only would removing him be a significant victory, but the information and intelligence that might be secured from a successful operation against his base could lead to valuable breakthroughs in the campaign against other al-Qaeda leaders.

Once again, the same combination of sophisticated tracking technology and coordinated raids that had proved so successful in the rescue of Norman Kember and the Christian Peacemaker hostages had come through with the intelligence they needed. In the early hours of 16 April, the SAS, backed up by the Paras, made their move.

As the Support Group kept the area secure against possible counter-attacks, two teams of commandos would storm the farmhouse; above them, snipers in Lynx helicopters would not only oversee the whole operation, but also be ready to pick off any escaping insurgents missed by the on-the-ground teams.

But if the element of surprise was crucial, it seemed it was also missing. As the SAS men slipped through the open door to the house, the terrorists were waiting for them.

◆ ◆ ◆

Three men went down under a storm of automatic gunfire almost immediately. Adapting with a speed and efficiency practised so often it had become instinct, the troopers following managed to grab them as they fell, dragging them back out of the building and withdrawing to the cover of the treeline, where medics could assess their condition. All had been hit, but none of the injuries were life-threatening.

Meanwhile, the building was no longer quiet. In what was beginning to look very much like a planned ambush, several of the enemy had run upstairs to the flat roof of the house; they now opened up on the SAS's position, spraying the area with AK-47s and lobbing grenades.

What was supposed to be a stealthy raid had become a full-on firefight.

It was time for the Paras to get involved. As they targeted the insurgents on the roof, the SAS used the distraction to once again move on the house. This time they entered more aggressively, launching grenades through the windows and announcing their entry with bursts of gunfire. As earlier, they were met with a volley of bullets in return, and two British men were hit before the shooter was taken out permanently.

As one of those wounded men received treatment, the other continued with the rest of the squad as they fanned out in two-man teams throughout the building. Another insurgent fell under fire in one room; in another, civilians – possibly the original owners of the farm – were found huddled in a corner; one woman was already dead, a further three plus a child were wounded. All were escorted from the building for questioning.

The ground floor secured, the squad moved on the stairs to the roof ... and from there things moved fast.

The team inside the building were rushed by a man wearing a suicide vest. As the commandos fired, he detonated the bomb, obliterating himself and blowing one of the troopers backwards. At the same time, another suicide bomber jumped from the house and rushed towards the medics treating the wounded – a sniper in one of the Lynx helicopters above picked him off before he could trigger his explosives. A third man in a bomb vest on the roof also blew himself up – but in his haste for martyrdom did so before any of the commandos were close enough for him to kill anyone but himself.

And then suddenly it was over. The house was clear. Five terrorists were confirmed dead – three by their own hands – and five SAS troopers were injured, though none seriously. Two more insurgents had been taken prisoner, hiding among the civilians escorted from the building.

◆ ◆ ◆

The original target was among the dead or captured men that night – but Operation Larchwood 4 turned up far more valuable prizes. One of the prisoners taken was a close associate of the religious advisor for Abū Muş'ab Zarqāwī, a Jordanian jihadist and prime target of the coalition forces. Known as the 'Sheikh of the Slaughterers', he had featured in numerous propaganda videos showing the torture and beheadings of hostages, and had assumed the mantle of al-Qaeda's de facto leader in Iraq. Also present in the building was a cache of photos, videos and other material related to al-Zarqawi ... all priceless intelligence in the effort to track him down.

Two months after Larchwood 4, that's exactly what they did. After pinpointing his location to another farmhouse north of Baghdad, two American F16 fighter-bombers dropped a brace of 500-pound (227-kg) bombs on the building, destroying everything – and everyone – within it.

OPERATION ELLAMY

LIBYA, MARCH–OCTOBER 2011

SADDAM HUSSEIN WAS not the only dictator in the Middle East, nor perhaps the most dangerous. Colonel Muammar Gaddafi seized power in Libya after a coup d'état in 1969, and subsequently presided over an increasingly brutal regime. Under his command Libya was responsible for a number of atrocities, most notably the attack on Pan Am Flight 103, in which a passenger jet flying from Frankfurt to Detroit was blown up. The plane exploded over the Scottish town of Lockerbie, killing all 259 on board, as well as eleven residents of the town: it is still classed as the deadliest terrorist attack in the history of the United Kingdom.

United Nations sanctions had been imposed on the regime throughout the 1980s and beyond, but in early 2011, what became known as the 'Arab Spring' changed the dynamic of the entire region – and marked the beginning of the end of Gaddafi's iron grip over the people of Libya.

British forces had been winding down their involvement in Iraq – on 30 April 2011 the UK formally ended all combat operations in the country – but meanwhile, and perhaps prompted or inspired by the fall of Saddam Hussein, popular uprisings had sprung up across the Arab world, most notably in Tunisia, Syria, Egypt and Libya.

Finding himself on the receiving end of the same kind of people-led revolution that had propelled him to power in the first place, Gaddafi's response was swift and merciless. In February 2011, as protests broke out in major cities across Libya, he announced that all rebels would be 'hunted down street by street, house by house'.

It was no idle threat. Gaddafi made use of his better-equipped forces to devastating effect, slaughtering protestors wherever they gathered, armed or otherwise: in a single incident in Benghazi that month, hundreds were killed when the army opened fire on a peaceful protest.

The United Nations response was equally swift ... and Britain was at the forefront. 'It is clear that this is an illegitimate regime that has lost the consent of its people,' Prime Minister David Cameron told the House of Commons, 'and our message to Colonel Gaddafi is simple: go now.'

In March, the United Nations Security Council passed a resolution allowing coalition forces including Britain to enforce a no-fly zone over Libya. Two Royal Navy destroyers and three frigates, along with squadrons of RAF Typhoon and Tornado fighter jets, were immediately deployed.

Officially, it was this massive display of firepower from the RAF and Royal Navy that destroyed Colonel Gaddafi's army – between them they took out over 200 armoured vehicles, artillery pieces and surface-to-air missiles – but in reality, another, secret war was being waged. And the SAS, unacknowledged and unofficial, were a central part of it.

After years of high-profile front-line operations in Iraq, the SAS was once again to be operating in the shadows, a hidden, clandestine weapon, a phantom menace. And it was doing so in Libya, exactly seventy years after its inception in the same deserts.

◆ ◆ ◆

The UN Security Council resolution that authorized military intervention against the Libyan regime by 'all necessary measures' also specifically disallowed the use of ground troops in the country, stating that 'a foreign occupation force of any form on any part of Libyan territory' was strictly prohibited.

However, even as the British bombing campaign – codenamed Operation Ellamy – inflicted huge losses on Gaddafi's army, it quickly became clear that air power alone was not going to defeat the dictator. On the ground the rebel forces were disorganized and lacked structure or proper tactical coherence, and despite the Western intervention, were failing to make serious headway. Gaddafi was still defiant. Even as the resolution was passed, he declared: 'We are coming tonight [for the rebels], and there will be no mercy.'

If Colonel Gaddafi's dictatorship were to be overthrown, the insurgents would need other help. No matter what the United Nations said.

The SAS's part in Operation Ellamy was highly confidential, highly clandestine, and, if not in direct contravention of the terms of the Security Council resolution, pushed the boundaries and bent the rules as far as was possible.

A secret unit of twenty men from 'D' Squadron, 22 SAS, had been deployed to Libya alongside the sanctioned bombing campaign, working on the ground with the rebels in the northern cities of Misrata and Brega as well as at a hidden training base in southern Libya.

Although the SAS played no active role in the civil war, those troopers were to be a crucial part of the rebellion. At the southern training base, they instructed the insurgents – the vast majority of whom had no military experience or training whatsoever – on basic combat techniques, as well as tactics and fieldwork exercises.

Seven decades of covert operations in the field, fighting against enemies that often held superior numbers and firepower, had made the SAS unequalled when it came to drilling a small force in how to strike hard and effectively against a larger power. Under their guidance, what had essentially been an enthusiastic and unorganized militia became a disciplined army capable of taking, securing and holding vital tactical positions, territories and even cities against Gaddafi's troops.

Similarly, working with the rebel leaders, the SAS men advised them on setting up a proper command infrastructure that could oversee and coordinate the entire campaign, as well as put in place the kind of protocols and arrangements that would ensure that when they did overthrow the dictator, the country would not collapse into the kind of lawlessness and factional fighting that had befallen Iraq.

Their position on the ground also helped coordinate air strikes to ensure maximum effect, and in August, this combination of better-focused bombing and newly invigorated and trained rebel ground forces saw the insurgents storm – and hold – the capital Tripoli.

Gaddafi himself fled to his hometown of Sirte, but he could not escape the SAS. Even as the rebels took Tripoli, another force under the guidance of the British commandos was moving from Misrata towards Sirte. On 20 October, following coordinated air strikes and a ground attack, Gaddafi was finally captured, and died of his injuries on the way to hospital.

Officially, the SAS were never in Libya, and even after a BBC report uncovered the truth the following year, the British government held firm to the line that their role as advisors and observers did not contravene the terms of the Security Council resolution.

Would the Libyan revolution have succeeded and Muammar Gaddafi been deposed without the 'advice and observation' of the SAS? Perhaps; perhaps not. Would the confrontation have extended far beyond its ten months and into a long and bloody war of attrition without their intervention? Almost certainly.

The history books record that the Libyan Civil War was won by a people's army rising up against a brutal dictator, assisted by a massive British-led bombing campaign. But what the history books don't reveal is that it was also arguably won by twenty men from 'D' Squadron, 22 SAS … without firing a shot in anger.

OPERATION JUBILEE

AFGHANISTAN, 2 JUNE 2012

FREEZING AND BRUISED, starving and terrified, British aid worker Helen Johnston had been kept hostage for eleven days in a cave complex in a barren waste of northern Afghanistan known as 'the Valley of the Ants'. She had been kidnapped along with a Kenyan medic and their two Afghan companions as they travelled by donkey though the remote Badakhshan province near the border with Tajikistan, and – dazed and delirious though she was – she was acutely aware that their chances of surviving the ordeal were slipping away with every day that passed.

She knew her captors were Taliban. She had heard them making their demands and was well aware that the British and Afghan governments had a firm policy of non-negotiation with kidnappers. She knew also that their threats to kill her were not made idly; they would do so if they didn't get their way.

What she did not know was that just 5 miles (8 km) away, a squad of men from 22 SAS were moving, silent and determined and at speed through the thick forests, towards the Valley of the Ants, prepared to risk their own lives to try to save hers.

What was to follow over the next few hours of Helen Johnston's life would be one of the riskiest and most famous SAS operations in modern history.

◆ ◆ ◆

The Black Hawk helicopters had left Bagram airbase just after midnight, skimming low above the treeline as they powered north towards the Tajikistan border. In one was a force of US Navy Seals; in the other a team from 22 SAS.

The commandos travelled light. This was to be an in-and-out operation, a clear target and a clear objective. Each carried MP5 automatic machine guns, Browning sidearms and grenades, as well as daggers tucked into their boots in case things got up close and personal. Several of the men were also equipped with sniper rifles.

Backup would follow at a discreet distance – Apache attack helicopters and a squadron of Afghan commandos – but they were to remain in reserve until needed. The key to success did not lie in greater numbers or bigger weapons, but in stealth, surprise and superior training.

Screw any of those up and the results could be catastrophic.

After a little over an hour the choppers set down again, in a rare clearing in the forest, some 5 miles (8 km) from the eventual target. They dared not go closer – even at night the forests and mountains of Badakhshan were alive with unfriendly eyes and ears: this was Taliban land, and their scouts and spies were everywhere. Even a distant whirr of an American helicopter blade would be enough to alert the enemy to their presence and see the ambushers become the ambushed.

The men unloaded and moved off without pausing, hitting a steady pace despite the tangle and snags of the forest's thick undergrowth. Bare slivers of the waxing moonlight filtered through the trees, but despite the gloom the men did not hesitate. The drone reconnaissance had been clear enough; maps and compass bearings committed to memory. They knew exactly where they were going and they travelled in as straight a line as possible towards it.

It was thanks to those Predator drones that the SAS and Navy Seals were here at all. In the days following the kidnap of Helen Johnston and her fellow aid workers, an immediate search for them began, high in the skies above north-eastern Afghanistan.

The four hostages had been in Afghanistan with the Swiss-based Christian charity Medair, helping administer basic medical care to the isolated valley villages of Badakhshan province, when, on 22 May, as they travelled between clinics, terrorists wielding Kalashnikov automatic machine guns had snatched them. Blindfolded and bound, they were taken into a bandit stronghold in the Valley of the Ants, and hidden in a network of caves carved out of the mountains.

From the moment their captors made their first demands – the release of a local militia leader, a notorious people-trafficker known as Jallah, plus US$11 million and the cessation of all Western aid activities in the area – Predator drones were launched above Badakhshan.

As the kidnappers continued to issue threats and demands – and the Afghan government refused to accede to any of them – the drones scanned the area for miles around the aid workers' last known location, simultaneously sweeping for mobile phone signals that might indicate the terrorists' hidden base.

After eight days they finally got the breakthrough they were praying for. As one of the kidnappers issued yet another demand, the surveillance team got a lock on the transmission: now not only was their location revealed, but special forces were able to listen in on their other conversations too.

A plan began to be put together. At a series of COBRA meetings in London, Prime Minister David Cameron was briefed by senior figures from the Ministry of Defence and MI6, as well as US military officials working with the International Security Assistance Force in Afghanistan.

Their analysis of the situation was grim. Taliban kidnappers were notoriously volatile and had no qualms about murdering their hostages in cold blood if they felt their demands were not being taken seriously. With zero progress being made through peaceful negotiations, the window for an extraction attempt was fast closing.

The prime minister's mind was made up for him the following day. A mobile phone intercept uncovered a conversation between the terrorists and a Taliban chief in which he urged the kidnappers to put on a 'show of intent' to demonstrate their seriousness.

A show of intent.

In the language of terrorism, that was shorthand for a public execution. A videotaped murder of one of the hostages, released to the media to press home the strength of their conviction.

On the afternoon of Friday 1 June, the order was given. The SAS, with backup from the Navy Seals, would follow the Predator drone intelligence to the Valley of the Ants. They would engage the kidnappers, attempt to rescue Helen Johnston and the other three captives, and do so immediately.

The Black Hawks flew from Bagram at midnight; at a little before 02.00 hours the rescuers had emerged from the forest and taken up positions under cover of the boulders and rockfall debris on the edge of the cave complex.

From there, they split up. Intelligence indicated that the four prisoners had been separated and were being kept in two different locations approximately a mile (1.6 km) apart, and guarded by anything up to ten terrorists at each site. The Americans would take one target; the SAS the other. Both forces would attack simultaneously.

As it turned out, the signal to strike was prompted by events on the ground. As the SAS watched through night-vision goggles, two guards emerged yawning from the caves. Seizing the moment, troopers with sniper rifles squeezed their triggers. Both were felled instantly.

The kills were clean, but the element of surprise was lost. Despite the ungodly hour, it seemed the Taliban were on high alert – and within seconds, further fighters emerged, responding with automatic gunfire and grenades hurled towards the British position. The battle was on.

As the SAS engaged the terrorists, the Navy Seals team launched their own attack. Infiltrating the cave complex without being seen, they rushed in on the shocked Taliban fighters. Bursts of fire lit up the dark caverns; almost before they had time to react seven of the insurgents lay dead. The Americans left them where they lay, continuing into the mountain, clearing the area, searching for the hostages.

They were nowhere to be seen.

Meanwhile, the SAS were moving fast. Not knowing if any of the prisoners were still alive, or in the caves at all, they fanned out and pushed forward with renewed urgency, assaulting the enemy from two fronts. Two more were despatched at the cave entrance, a fifth was killed inside. Finally, the gunfire stopped.

As the smoke cleared, four more bodies could be seen in the complex, hidden in the shadows at the back of the caves.

SAS troopers moved cautiously forward, MP5s trained, while others covered them from the rear ... and then one of the figures called out.

A woman's voice, speaking English. Helen Johnston was alive.

◆ ◆ ◆

Within minutes, all four hostages were escorted from the caves, loaded into helicopters, and, as quickly and efficiently as they came, the SAS and Navy Seals were gone again, speeding through the Afghan night back to Bagram.

Twelve terrorists had been killed without the special forces soldiers sustaining a single casualty; and, most importantly, the kidnapped aid workers had all been rescued alive and unharmed. It was a stunning success.

Operation Jubilee was an example of the SAS at their bravest, boldest and deadliest, and another uncompromising message to terrorists and kidnappers. Wherever in the world you are, however many men or weapons you have, whatever fanatical beliefs you hold, if you cross the SAS, you will pay a terrible price.

From infiltrating airfields in North Africa to spreading havoc among the Nazi occupiers of France and Italy; from holding back armies in the jungles of Malaysia to defending impossible positions in Oman; from daring hostage rescues in Mogadishu, Sierra Leone, Baghdad and the heart of London to combating the IRA in Northern Ireland; from wartime operations in the South Atlantic and Iraq to bringing war criminals to justice in the former Yugoslavia, and in countless other operations in the fractured post-9/11 world, the SAS have been – and continue to be – Britain's greatest, most secret and most effective weapon.

On the day after the rescue, Prime Minister David Cameron addressed the media from 10 Downing Street, and paid tribute to an elite special force unmatched anywhere in the world. 'We will never be able to publish their names, but the whole country should know we have an extraordinary group of people who work for us who do amazingly brave things,' he said.

He also issued a stark warning to terrorists everywhere. 'They should know if they take British citizens hostage, we do not pay ransoms, we do not trade prisoners. They can expect a swift and brutal end.'

Who dares wins.

BIBLIOGRAPHY

In researching the exploits of the SAS men and their missions, the author is indebted to the following books, websites and resources.

Books

Briscoe, Charles Harry, *All Roads Lead to Baghdad: Army Special Operations Forces in Iraq*, Military Bookshop (2013).

Cole , Roger and Belfield, Richard, *SAS Operation Storm: Nine Men Against Four Hundred*, Hodder & Stoughton (2011).

Dickens, Peter, *SAS: Secret War in South East Asia*, Frontline (1997).

Lewis, Damien, *SAS Italian Job*, Quercus (2018).

Lewis, Jon E., *SAS: The Autobiography*, Robinson Publishing (2011).

McIntyre, Ben, *SAS: Rogue Heroes*, Penguin (2016).

McNab, Andy, *Bravo Two Zero*, Bantam (1993).

Moreno, Isidoro J. Ruiz, *Comandos en acción: El Ejército en Malvinas*, Emece Editores (1986).

Mortimer, Gavin, *SAS Combat Vehicles 1942–91*, Osprey (2021).

Mortimer, Gavin, *The SAS in World War II: An Illustrated History*, Osprey (2011).

Ryan, Chris, *The One That Got Away*, Century (1995).

SAS Regimental Association, *The SAS War Diary 1941–45* (2011).

Thatcher, Margaret, *The Downing Street Years*, Harper Press (1993).

Urban, Mark, *Task Force Black: The Explosive True Story of the SAS and the Secret War in Iraq*, Abacus (2010).

Websites

Weaponsandwarfare.com

Warfarehistorynetwork.com

British Resistance Archive at staybehinds.com

Eliteukforces.info

Other sources

The National Army Museum and The Imperial War Museum.

SAS – Embassy Siege, broadcast 8 Jan 2003 (BBC documentary)

INDEX